Ella Church

Artistic embroidery;

Containing practical instructions in the ornamental branches of

needlework - Vol. 1

Ella Church

Artistic embroidery;
Containing practical instructions in the ornamental branches of needlework - Vol. 1

ISBN/EAN: 9783337727000

Printed in Europe, USA, Canada, Australia, Japan

Cover: Foto ©ninafisch / pixelio.de

More available books at **www.hansebooks.com**

Vol. III. No. 192.

THE LEISURE HOUR LIBRARY

May 26, 1888. Published Weekly. Annual Subscription, $1.50.
Entered at the Post Office, New York, as Second Class Matter.
Copyright, 1887, by F. M. Lupton.

ARTISTIC EMBROIDERY

By **ELLA RODMAN CHURCH.**

F. M. LUPTON, Publisher
63 Murray Street, N. Y.

ARTISTIC EMBROIDERY:

Containing Practical Instructions

IN THE

Ornamental Branches

OF

NEEDLEWORK,

WITH NEARLY TWO HUNDRED ILLUSTRATIONS AND EXPLANATORY DIAGRAMS.

BY

ELLA RODMAN CHURCH

PUBLISHED FOR THE TRADE.

CHAPTER I.

WORSTED EMBROIDERY.

EMBROIDERY has been defined as "the art of adding to the surface of woven textures a representation of any object we wish to depict, through the medium of the needle, threaded with the material in which the work is to be executed."

From the earliest times, it has been the amusement of women of leisure, and the occupation of those whose skilful fingers must be used to bring in returns of daily bread. In the Middle Ages, a regular work-room, or "studio," was set apart for this especial purpose in the dim old castle; and there the whole paraphernalia of embroidery-frames, materials, and implements, were always to be found. There, too, the chatelaine sat with her maidens embroidering cushions, or book-covers, or those wonderful pieces of historical tapestry afterward displaced by the more mechanical arras.

"Tapestry richly wrought
And woven close,"

was the favorite needlework of those days; and these hangings, or "veils," were rendered necessary by the style of building, which afforded many convenient chinks and loopholes for the wind. Some of these ancient pieces of embroidery were very rich, the designs being worked with worsted or silk of various colors, and often mixed with gold or silver threads, on canvas, cloth, or silk.

The oldest specimen of this kind of work now in existence is the famous tapestry of Bayeux—the work of the English Matilda and her attendants. A piece of embroidery over two hundred and twenty feet long, although not much more than half a yard wide, is no trifling accomplishment; and in spite of the red, blue, green, and yellow horses, some of them with two legs of a different color from the rest of their bodies, one cannot but reverence this curious triumph of the needle that can claim eight centuries of birthdays. It is entirely worked with worsted in very little variety of coloring, as the Norman princess had few advantages of this sort, but she has represented to the best of her ability the invasion and conquest of England by Duke William and his followers. The battle of Hastings is ingeniously emphasized by a bordering composed of the bodies of the slain.

Few would have the time or the inclination for such a piece of work in these days; and "some of our moderns are inclined to think that, in days of old, when the chief employment of a woman's life was needlework, she must have had a very dull, dreary, monotonous time of it. But when we survey ancient heirlooms, veritable works of art —the smooth, mossy crewel-work, the frost-like point-lace, the shining gold-threaded ecclesiastical work, or even the conventional forms of the now despised cross-stitch—we imagine every happiness and beauty connected with the age of chivalry, as we are conscious of a sense of wonder akin to that felt on beholding some magnificent ancient jewels, or plate, or pictures."

As late as the days of the *Spectator*, it was written: "How memorable would that matron be who should have it inscribed on her monument that she wrought out the whole Bible in tapestry, and died in a good old age, after having covered three hundred yards of wall in the Mansion House"—but no such exploit is on record.

The most fashionable worsted embroidery of the present time is

CREWEL-WORK.

This style of work was much in vogue during the latter part of the eighteenth century, and has recently been revived, and the *modus operandi* dignified by the name of the South Kensington stitch. But people with great-grandmothers produce pieces of work done in a similar manner; and the stitch is the same as the long stitch in silk embroidery, only longer and more careless.

Crewel work was brought to such a state of perfection by the famous Miss Linwood, who literally painted pictures with her needle from her thirteenth until her seventy-eighth year, copying the old masters so successfully that, at a little distance, the needle-worked picture could not be distinguished from the painted one, that every one wanted to imitate her; but few having the same gift, this branch of art fell into disrepute.

Miss Linwood's pictures were marvels of patience and skill. They were embroidered on a stiff, twilled fabric called "tammy," on which the outline was drawn in chalk; and the entire ground was covered with close, irregular stitches, of great fineness in the more delicate touches. The shading was perfect, the crewels being dyed under the artist's own supervision; and her first needle-painting, the "Salvator Mundi," from Carlo Dolci, was wonderfully true to the original.

Her collection, which was exhibited for some time in London, contained sixty-four pieces; and among them was a portrait of herself in the bloom of youth and beauty.

The great beauty of crewel-work is its freedom from set rules; in taking the stitches, the needle is used more like the brush in the hand of the artist.

THE CREWEL STITCH

resembles the wrong side of long back-stitching more than anything else; and is illustrated by Figures 1 and 2.

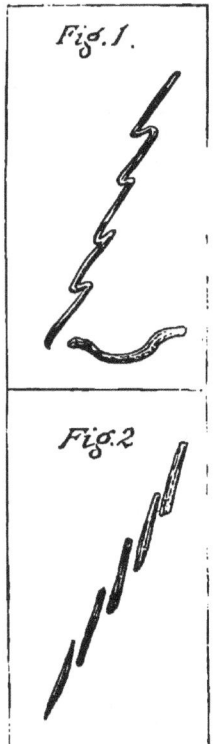

The needle is put in at the back of the material and brought out at 1, put in again at 2 and brought out at 3, put in again at 4 and brought out at 5, and so on to the end of the line. In outline-work the thread should be kept to the left of the needle, and great care taken to bring the needle up exactly in the line of the pattern, or a wavy, uncertain outline will be the result, and the character of the pattern will be lost.

This method of working is to be used when the material is put in a frame; but when the work is done in the hand, it is best illustrated by Figure 2. The easiest and quickest way in this case is to begin at the bottom and work upward—putting the needle through (from the back) at 1, and back again at 2—through again at 3, and back at 4—until the entire distance has been traversed.

It will be seen that the stitch is very simple, and that much is left to the discretion of the worker. Care must be taken that the worsted is not pulled too tight, nor left too loose, as the effect must be smooth and even—with the curves clearly defined, and the points sharp and complete.

In ordinary crewel-work, the stitch should be from three-eighths to half an inch long, according to its position—some stitches must necessarily be shorter—as in filling in, they must dovetail into each other like the tiles of a roof, that no sharp line of color may indicate the different shades. To produce the desired effect, all the stitches should not be taken close up to the inner edge of color. Figures 3 and 4 will give some idea of this shading.

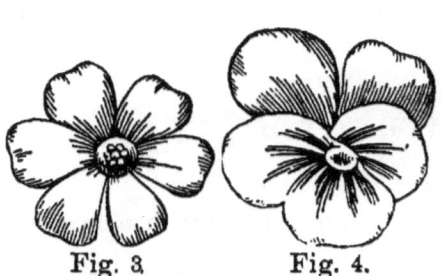

Fig. 3.   Fig. 4.

A leaf or stalk should never be worked across, but always (and the same rule, of course, applies to flower-petals) in the same direction as the fibres in a natural leaf. With such leaves as brambles, and others that will suggest themselves, one side should be a darker shade than the other. Figure 5 shows the natural way of working a leaf.

In working the stalk of a flower, it is better to begin at the lower end first, and work on the outline until it is crossed by a leaf or terminates in a flower; then pass the needle to the other side, and work back again to the lower end; then work another line of stitches *inside* the outline till the stalk is filled up. See Figure 6. Leaves of one shade are done in the same way, and the veins are put in last.

Crewel-work has many recommendations; it is easy, is done with comparatively little labor, and yet it affords scope for the exercise of artistic skill of the highest order. A great variety of beautiful shades may be had, and the worsted washes beautifully, thus possessing a decided advantage over many other styles of ornamentation. The materials are also quite inexpensive, and taking it altogether, it produces the best effects with the least outlay of labor and expense of any other kind of embroidery.

Floral designs suit this style of work best; and somewhat conventionalized models are most suitable—flowers that can be expressed by the fewest lines in form and the fewest shades in color. Daisy-shaped flowers are particularly suitable; and the well known sunflower, not *too* much conventionalized, but with the tendency of its long petals to droop a little just indicated here and there, is represented in Figure 7.

Fig. 5.

Simple, old-fashioned flowers are most successful in crewel-work. Wild roses being simple, and having very distinct petals and well marked centres, are better than the double and treble triumphs of the florist—to which painting alone can do justice. The daffodil, narcissus, and lily tribes, with primroses, honeysuckles, pansies, and daisies, bloom out charmingly in crewels; and almost any clearly defined leaf is pleasing.

Butterflies and vases may also be successfully introduced, but the atter should be chiefly in outline.

Fig. 6.

The experienced crewel worker may study nature for designs, and discover unending combinations of beauty and delicate touches of detail which give a character to the whole. In the veining of leaves especially this is shown; and the leaf of the common scarlet poppy, veined and unveined, in Figures 8 and 9, will show how much depends on careful finish.

But embroidery in general should not attempt too much detail—a thorn here and there on a rose-stem being sufficient to suggest the thorny nature of roses, while only a few of the larger serrations of the leaves should be retained. The bramble, when shorn of superfluous outline, is a very desirable leaf for embroidery; and Figure 10 shows it in its natural state, which, if worked,

Fig. 7

would be a confused mass of nothing in particular—while in Figure

11, its shape and general character are preserved, but all unnecessary notchings and veinings are pruned away.

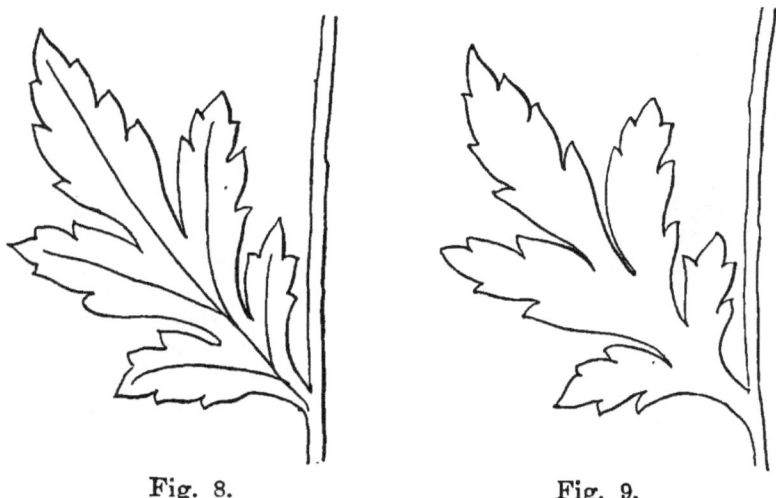

Fig. 8.   Fig. 9.

An important point in embroidery is to know what may be to advantage left undone; and as crewel-work is entirely free from all artificial raising, it is merely suggestive of general form.

The crewel itself is a particularly strong, twisted woollen yarn, quite unlike zephyr and the other wools in use. The shades of color are very soft and numerous, and blend beautifully in delicate flower-petals and varying leaves. The work is usually done on heavy linen sheeting, as this wears well, is easily washed, and is particularly suitable for tidies, doilies, and many small articles.

Other materials may be used to advantage; but cloth, velvet, or silk is not suitable for crewel-work. Serge makes a very nice foundation; and a pair of invalid's slippers, made lately, were worked on white *felt*. But these were done in Canada, where many materials are to be had which cannot be found here. Said slippers were merely to thrust the toes in, as all the rest was sole; and this white felt pointed piece was orna-

Fig. 10.

mented with strawberries in crewel-work. This beautiful fruit is quite as effective as flowers are; and in Figure 12 the clusters may be used separately, or continued indefinitely for a border. A very pretty footstool could be made by grouping them closely for the top, and putting the bordering on the band. The fruit may be either red or white as best suits the groundwork.

Velveteen makes a good background for crewel embroidery; and this is suitable both for footstools and hangings. It is also handsome for mantel lambrequins. But the favorite material is crash towelling—which is so generally used for the purpose that crewels seem inseparable from it, and the work is quite as often called "crash-work" as crewel-work. Crash is very serviceable for tidies, toilet covers, toilet mats, travelling bags, etc.; but it does not hang in graceful folds for curtains and portières, and it is not worthy of being embroidered in silks.

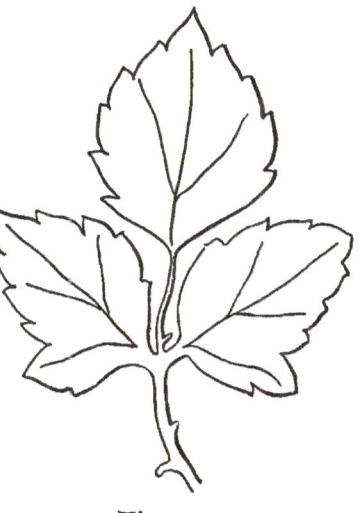

Fig. 11.

There is a ribbed velveteen in different shades of drab and brown, which looks remarkably well as a foundation for crewel-work, if the latter is done in a rich, bold design. It should be remembered, as a general thing, that while rich materials may be used on cheap groundwork, worsted embroidery is very unsuitable on a rich foundation.

We have attempted suggestions only in the way of patterns, as these may be bought in great variety wherever the crewels are sold; and for those who are unable to design from nature this will be found a great convenience.

It is not long since all worsted work was done in mechanical patterns on canvas; and some of this work, with stitches laid as regularly as minute mosaics, and the shades blended as by the hand of an artist, is still very beautiful. It is the mosaic-work of embroidery, and bears the same relation to it that the real mosaic does to painting; but crewel-work has the advantage of being more quickly done, and of expressing better the individuality of the worker. How quickly, for instance, with needle and crewels, the very essence of a May morning may be condensed into the cluster of apple-blossoms from the laden bough beside the window; but who could extemporize them into a pattern of set squares on the spur of the moment?

ARTISTIC EMBROIDERY.

ARTICLES TO BE WORKED IN CREWELS.

It is always more satisfactory in a work of this kind to find some practical illustrations of the suggestions given; and many people like to know exactly what to make. We shall be more explicit, therefore, in this little volume than would be possible in one of greater pretension; and mention articles to be made, as far as our limits will permit.

Being quickly done and effective at a distance, crewel-embroidery is very suitable for large pieces of work, such as curtains, portières, friezes, and so forth. Portières and friezes have a pleasant suggestion about them of old tapestries; and the latter are really wall-valances. One would scarcely undertake

AN EMBROIDERED FRIEZE

even in crewel-work, for a large apartment; but a moderate-sized room could be adorned with this wall drapery without an unreasonable outlay of time. Claret-colored serge, or velveteen, if in harmony with the other coloring of the room, worked with perpendicular sunflowers or lilies (Figure 13 is a good pattern for the latter), with a bordering of gold-color and green at top and bottom, would be very ornamental. The frieze could be finished with a fringe and hang loose at the lower edge, which is prettier, or fastened at both sides, paper-fashion.

Colors and figures may be varied indefinitely—for the lattter, a standing army of storks would often be preferred. Dragons, too, are now so generally regarded as cheerful domestic animals in the way of adornment, that a procession of them across the walls of an apartment on an elaborate frieze would, doubtless, add a pleasing element in the way of decoration. But those who say, Give me beauty, or give me nothing, in the way of ornament, will prefer designs of flowers and leaves.

A DADO IN CREWELS

Fig. 12.

may be done in the same way, only that there

is more of it; and being nearer the eye, the design should be more close and elaborate. The patterns on rich papers will be found suggestive studies; and it may be remembered that the material for groundwork can be adapted to the purse of the embroiderer and the other belongings of the apartment, from velveteen at a dollar a yard to crash-towelling at ten cents.

The wide material known as jute, and just the least bit in the style of brown straw-matting, would make a very nice dado worked in crewels, with a darker brown picked out with gold color; and this same material hangs in graceful folds for curtains and portières. A brown room could be made very beautiful in this way; and quiet

Fig. 13.

though it is, there is a richness about brown that is always suggestive of gilding.

A WORSTED-WORKED PORTIÈRE

should be of velveteen, if this harmonizes with the other hangings of the room, as the material has a particularly rich effect in doorways, and artistically executed crewel-work suits it admirably. Brown velveteen with golden sunflowers, or gray with wild roses, or dark blue with lilies, will be found very handsome.

In working portières, it is necessary to remember that they should be well covered with embroidery, because the light falls on all their parts; while an embroidered border suffices for curtains, as the edges only are likely to catch the sun's rays.

Other hangings may be made for the open shelves of cabinets and étagères ; these should also harmonize with the general decoration of the room in color and style, but may be richer and more elaborate than the larger pieces of embroidery, as they will be subjected to closer inspection.

CURTAINS WITH SPRAYS OF SUMAC.

These were really beautiful. The ground was a pale sage green, in perfect keeping with the prevailing hue of the room; and the soft bright shades of the crewels were so delicately blended, that the effect was a perfect needle-painting of these bright-hued darlings of the autumn. They were embroidered on the plain band of the sage—colored material that formed the simple cornice—down the front of the curtains, and here and there, on the body of the drapery, a spray seemed to have dropped by accident.

A SWEET-PEA TABLE COVER

which emanated from the same hand, was also a thing of beauty. The table was a round one of moderate size, and the top was tightly covered with maroon-colored flannel. A straight band of white flannel between two narrow strips of the maroon formed the border, and on this white ground the sweet peas were worked in delicately-tinted crewels. Feather-stitching, of black and bright green, marked the joining of the white flannel to the maroon on either side. The bordering was fastened to the table with silver-headed nails, and finished with a worsted fringe to match the maroon flannel.

This beautiful work was all copied from natural models during hours of summer leisure on a country piazza, and many beautiful thoughts and memories were wrought into the bright-hued leaves and petals.

SCREENS IN CREWEL-WORK.

We saw a honeysuckle screen lately, that might have been beautiful, but was not because it had altogether too sombre an air to be viewed in the light of an ornament. The workmanship was fine, and regularly done according to the rules of art, but as the ground was black and the coral honeysuckle was represented in very dull reds and greens, the effect was not enlivening. A gray ground of a silver tinge would have been a great improvement, but dark work on a dark ground is a dismal production.

The woodbine honeysuckle can be reproduced in crewels in very natural colors, and we have seen some that almost diffused a June odor about them. They were worked on very fine, soft crash, and intended for a tidy; but a beautiful fire-screen could be made of them on a blue or plum-colored ground.

The large folding-screens, so often in strips of coarse Berlin-wool work, are very handsome in crewels; and climbing vines of all kinds are particularly suited to them. A crimson ground with water-lilies in one corner, and the wild morning-glory, with its nearly white blossoms (that grows in damp places and therefore harmonizes with the water-lily) trailing its beautiful length across the largest space, while the inevitable heron, balanced, of course, on one foot, stands sentinel among his reeds and rushes, where classic cat-tails bristle like spears, is *vis-à-vis* to the water-lilies on the other side, would be found bright in coloring and handsome in effect.

But a screen that looks as if some one had come in and thrown a handful of daisies over it may be quite as pretty, and is certainly less work.

CARRIAGE WRAPS

of fine crash, ornamented with crewel-work, are handsome and serviceable for warm weather. A bordering of strawberries and leaves near the edge, or one of periwinkle with its delicate blue flowers, would be very pretty; and this bordering, with a large monogram in the centre, would sufficiently ornament the article.

But endless are the uses to which this simple and charming style of embroidery may be put; and the suggestions given may be indefinitely multiplied and rearranged in various forms.

CHAPTER II.

SIMPLE IDEAS OF COLOR.

BEFORE proceeding to silk embroidery, it may be well to consider some simple rules of color, as the proper arrangement of color is of far greater importance than the regular placing of stitches, and no embroidery can be artistic without it.

An old-fashioned poet gives some good advice on this subject:

> " Choose such judicious force of shade and light,
> As suits the theme and satisfies the sight;
> Weigh part with part, and with prophetic eye
> The future power of all thy tints descry."

Truth in rhyme was never better brought out than in the following lines:

> " Know first that light displays and shade destroys
> Refulgent Nature's variegated dyes;
> Thus bodies near the light distinctly shine
> With rays direct, and as it fades decline."

An eye for color is of the same nature as an ear for music—one knows intuitively what is right; but this is by no means a very common gift; and there are some rules to be observed, independently of the guidance of taste, that are within the reach of all.

Thus scarlet and yellow were never intended for close companions; brown or lilac invariably quarrel with a scarlet ground; blue and green together, or yellow and green, are like an unpleasant taste in the mouth; blue is perfectly amiable with *écru* (the French name for all the drabs and fawns); a cold green blue may be successfully paired with lilac; drabs with a rich brown tone in them take kindly to yellow; pink and gray are as harmonious as love-birds; scarlet affably locks arms with slate-green and red-brown; green with maize, and also with some shades of salmon; blue and maize were made for each other; lilac and green, blue and claret, are also devoted couples.

One who knows says that black should never be used next a high light; one-eighth of every object has a high light upon it, one-eighth is darkest shadow, and six parts light, or half-tint. No objects in nature are *positively* blue, red, or yellow, owing to two causes: one, that most objects reflect the sky; the other, that the atmosphere between the eyes of the observer and the light causes the brightness of the tints to be deadened. So that care must be taken to avoid the immediate contact of bright colors with each other when an attempt is made to imitate nature.

Shaded embroidery should be guided by the same rules that apply to water-color painting, except that greater depth and brilliancy, and consequently less delicacy, are the results in view. It requires much discrimination to give a natural hue to leaves, and, at the same time, to produce such contrasts as will give the proper relief. Portions of each should be much lighter than others; and in the grouping, a mass should be thrown into shadow under the bright leaves—the shadow being composed of dark green mixed with neutral tint.

Much may be learned in the way of color by study and observation; but to get just the right shades of even harmonious colors requires care and skill. Thus simple red may be used with pure green; but scarlet, which is red tinged with yellow, must have a blue green; crimson, which is red tinged with blue, a yellow green. All colors are darker on a light ground and lighter on a dark ground, so that tints should be selected according to the groundwork.

Position, too, must be considered; a piece of embroidery that is intended for a dark corner should have brighter colors and stronger contrasts than one which is to be placed in a full light. On a white ground very delicate tints are most suitable, while the broken grays of crash will harmonize livid colors.

Masses of blue should be avoided, as blue is a cold color; and white requires skilful management, as it should be shaded off delicately by means of tints that have a large portion of white in their composition. But all flowers of the same kind should not be worked in the same shades of color; three white flowers, for instance, of the same species and in one cluster, requiring eight shades of silk or worsted to embroider them properly, should have these shades differently arranged. For one, a greater portion of the five lightest tints would be used; for the next, the middle shades, perhaps; in the third, the darkest would be most prominent; all this would depend on the position of the flowers and the skill of the embroiderer.

Many different colors in one piece of work spoil the effect, except in particular cases; some one prevailing color should be adopted, and the rest chosen with reference to it. Some of the most beautifully colored work is done in one key of color: one color being taken as the key-note, and those shades only are used that form its component parts, or that have the original color in their composition. On gold-colored satin, for instance, nothing looks so well as a design colored in shades of russet and golden browns, introducing every now and then a lighter or darker shade of the pure ground color.

In taking green for the ground color, if a yellow green, then the highest note should be yellow; and it should be carried down through all the brown, warm, and russet greens, which owe all their warmth to yellow. If the ground is a blue green, colder greens must be used, of a sage rather than a russet tint, while the key-note is struck with a pure blue. Under this restraint, the effect, though subdued, is very agreeable.

If a pure blue is placed near a pure yellow, the effect is glaring; but when the blue is slightly toned with yellow and the yellow with blue, there is quite a different result. A strong blue and a bright red, with a yellow gleam in it, stare each other out of countenance; but a subdued russet-green as a neighbor makes them harmonious.

Purples, and all shades inclining to blue, are difficult to dispose satisfactorily—those with the least blue in them are preferable. Russet is one part blue, one part yellow, and two parts red; olive, one part blue, two parts yellow, and one part red. It is more pleasing than slate, which has two parts blue, one part yellow, and one red.

When the ground is a *red* plum or maroon, pure red pinks, with no shade of blue in them, will be much more harmonious than blue; but if the ground is a *blue* plum, pale blue will be better than pink. The shading of flowers is always in different shades of the same color; and this method applied to embroidery produces the most charming results. A pattern worked on a dark ground in a lighter shade of the same color is always pleasing; and in a small room especially a great variety of colors should be avoided. A crimson room should have chair or table cover, or tidy, in *pale* crimson mingled with a little pink of the same tone.

Thus after a pretty conceit, one room might be called the rose-room, being furnished with the crimson heart of that beautiful flower running through the shades of pink suggestively in the lighter portions, and "broidered over" with roses and buds where ornament is desirable; another might be the sunflower-room, with its warm golden browns and gleams of yellow, and the honest full-moon face of that plebeian blossom astonished at being "done" in silks and crewels, and set up to be looked at; while the morning-glory-room, in grays and blues, should imprison all the sunshine to light up its cold colors, and afford a congenial resting-place for its pictured blossoms.

CHAPTER III.

SILK EMBROIDERY.

This beautiful work has been practised from the earliest times; and the ancient Egyptians particularly excelled in it. Much of this was done on linen—to which we shall refer afterward. The very sails of their galleys were embroidered; and their "divers colors of needlework on both sides" seems to mean that it was done so that the work was the same on the wrong side as on the right—a method of working that requires an immense amount of skill and patience, and which is now found only among those eminently painstaking races, the Chinese, Japanese, and Hindoos.

Silk embroidery is done on almost any material except cotton and coarse linen; but silk and velvet seem the most suitable fabrics for groundwork. If well done, it is handsome on anything; and as it is an expensive kind of needlework, great care should be taken in doing it. As a general thing it requires framing, and especially when floss-silk is used. Frames are of various kinds; the best for large pieces of work being the standing frame (see Figure 14), which has adjustable screws, and can be lowered or heightened at pleasure.

The hand or lap frame (Figure 15) is more convenient in embroidering smaller articles.

In putting work into the frame, a strip of strong tape or linen should be stitched along the woof ends of the material—which must then be firmly sewed with strong double thread to the webbing on the frame. It should be made as tight and firm as possible; the strain being increased gradually and cautiously until the tension appears to be sufficient. The woof ends should be braced to the side pieces with fine twine. A packing-needle threaded with twine must be drawn through the upper right-hand corner of the tape or linen, and the end securely tied. The twine must be sewn over the lath till the lower corner is reached, knotted securely, and cut off; the other side must then be done in the same manner.

When the material is larger than the frame, it may be sewed on to the bars and rolled round one of them, with tissue paper and wadding between to prevent the stuff from creasing; and when the part in the

20   ARTISTIC EMBROIDERY.

Fig. 14.

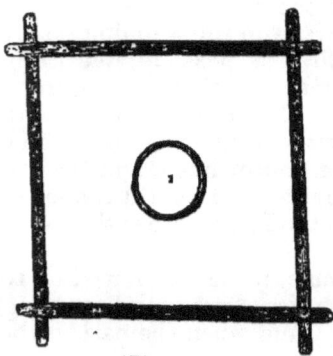

Fig. 15.

frame is finished, it is rolled round the opposite bar, and so on, until the whole is completed. The centre ring, marked 1, is a hand frame used for small pieces of embroidery.

In working with a frame it is desirable to use both hands—one to put the needle through from the outside, and the other to bring it up again from beneath. This will be slow work at first; but practice and patience will enable one to do it quite dextrously, and the great convenience of working in this way will fully repay the trouble of learning it. Two thimbles will be necessary, one for each hand.

THE STITCH FOR SILK EMBROIDERY
is the same as for crewel-work, except that it is shorter. Other stitches are often introduced, which will be noticed in their place; but the proper stitch for shaded embroidery, the most attractive of this fascinating work, is to draw the needle upward from the right and finish by putting it down to the left. The right hand

should always be above the frame, and the left beneath—making the stitches as long as the work will admit of their being, as the brilliancy of the silk is destroyed by crowded and short stitches.

Silk embroidery is both dainty and effective; and as the materials are expensive, great care should be used in doing the work, that it may not only give satisfaction at first, but prove sufficiently durable to repay the outlay of time and money. It is best to avoid touching the silk by drawing it through the fingers while working.

Anything like a regular embroidery stitch is to be avoided, except in those portions of the work where it is necessary; as the most charming effects are usually produced where there seems to have been the greatest indifference to mechanical regularity.

When the work has been properly arranged in the frame, the first step in artistic embroidery is to observe the position of the flowers and leaves—taking it for granted that the outlines have been properly traced—and if the model is of natural blossoms, so much the better. It is particularly advisable, before beginning the embroidery, to study the lights and shades; the edges and rounder parts, both of the leaves and petals of flowers, as they embrace more surface, naturally receive the light first and are worked with the palest tints.

In a group of flowers (see Figure 16) it is recommended to begin with the smaller parts, such as the stems, buds, and leaves; and great care should be taken to have every portion clearly outlined—although a visible outline should be avoided in filled-in work. Again, the careful blending of shades mentioned in crewel-work must be enforced—the stitches being so nicely placed to produce the right effect, that their beginning and ending are quite lost.

GROUP OF FLOWERS FOR SILK EMBROIDERY.

The stems of slender flowers should always be done in stalk-stitch, as they can be made more neatly and with less trouble than in satin-stitch. The centres are worked in French knot stitch. This is a pretty pattern for a variety of small articles: glove-box, letter-box, pincushion, case, etc. Or it may be enlarged for a footstool, sofa-cushion, or chair-seat.

In working leaves, one half should be done first; and great care taken to follow the direction of the fibres. Figure 17 shows the direction the lines would take if we were shading the leaf in drawing. In working a pansy the stitches should take the direction of the lines in Figure 18; and not *cross* the petals, as in Figure 19. Figure 20 shows the proper filling up of a thick stalk.

For narrow leaves, where one stitch will reach from the middle to the edge, it is best to pass the thread from the edge underneath to the middle—as this makes each stitch begin in the middle, and the under

22   ARTISTIC EMBROIDERY.

side is nearly the same as the upper. A broad leaf or petal requires more than one stitch between the middle and the edge; and for these, the needle may be brought up again wherever the next stitch seems to be wanted. But two together should not begin nor end on the same line—except on the outside edge to preserve the outline, or in showing the middle rib.

Fig. 16.

Unless the embroidery is very large and bold, the line formed by the meeting of the stitches down the middle of a leaf, as in Figure 21, will sufficiently mark the mid-rib. If in the real leaf it is very deep and plainly defined, a very narrow space between the two lines, tapering till the threads meet again near the point, will generally be sufficient. See Figure 22. Lateral veins need not usually be indicated at all; but if they are very marked, and of a different color from the leaf itself, they may be laid on by a cord or a piece of thick-silk twist— fastening it down with small stitches in silk of the same color. This must only be done in large and rather coarse work.

Fig. 17.

Another important point is the distinct bringing out of the different characters of the stalks. The three examples given (Figures 23, 24 and 25) will show how the different joinings vary, and that care must be taken to make these distinctions, as well as to finish them off properly. It has been well said that the difference between mechanical and artistic embroidery consists in showing judgment and finish in all these small matters.

Other stitches used in silk embroidery, besides the one known distinctively as embroidery-stitch, are satin-stitch, French-knot-stitch, stalk-stitch, point-russe, herring-bone or feather-stitch, ladder-stitch, chain-stitch, etc.

Satin-stitch is used a great deal in white embroidery, and many persons are familiar with it who have never attempted to work in colors. It is also called

Fig. 18.

FRENCH, OR FLAT EMBROIDERY.

The stitches lie smoothly in a diagonal direction close to each other—little or no attention to light or shade being necessary. It may be done very effectively in one color, and is then often enriched by gold or silver cord around the edges.

It looks best worked with Mitorse silk—which is also the most durable, as it does not fray in the wear nor so quickly lose its glossy appearance as when done with floss or Dacca silk. This work is suitable for articles of furniture and dress, as well as for small ornamental work.

Fig. 19.

Figure 26 is a good illlustration of flat embroidery in a pretty border pattern, which may be edged with gold thread or with silk of another color.

BORDER IN FLAT EMBROIDERY.

THE FRENCH KNOT.

This is very useful for the centres of such flowers as the daisy and sunflower, and for filling up leaves in a showy manner. It is made by bringing the thread through to the front of the work, and holding it in the left hand, four or five inches from the work—the needle being in the right hand; the thread is twisted two or three times around the needle as close to the work as possible; then the point is turned down into the material nearly, but not exactly, where the thread came up; the needle is pulled through to the other side, and the thread drawn carefully till the knot is firm. The thread must be drawn round the needle close up to the work before the needle is pulled quite through, lest the knot should hang loose and spoil the effect.

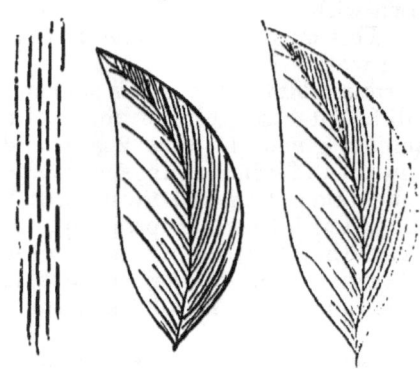

Fig. 20.   Fig. 21.   Fig. 22.

Fig. 23.   Fig. 24.   Fig. 25.

STALK-STITCH

Is very easily and quickly done. In veining leaves and working small stems, it is more manageable than any other stitch; and it is formed by making a straight stitch rather more than a sixteenth of an inch in length—then for the next stitch, putting the needle about half-way back into the first one and working it the same length.

This is so quickly done, that there is danger of doing it carelessly; but if properly worked, it resembles a finely-twisted cord, and gives a very neat finish to the embroidery.

Fig. 26.

POINT-RUSSE.

This is a stitch frequently mentioned in new embroidery; but the *modus operandi* does not seem to be so well known as that of many others. Possibly because of its very simplicity—for Point-Russe is merely a succession of back-stitches neatly and regularly done. It is used for many small articles; and is a useful adjunct in more artistic work.

The illustration in Figure 27 shows the effect, and the uses to which it can be put. Every line of the design must be carefully followed in

Fig. 27.

working it; and very pretty borderings and ornamental figures in long stitches are often made with it. Medallions are very pretty in Point-Russe; and we give one in Figure 28 that is worked entirely in this stitch, and made very effective in scarlet and gold. This is intended for a purse, and is worked on light brown leather or kid.

Figure 30 is also very pretty, and may be worked in one or more colors.

Figure 81 is a border pattern that is very effective. The diamonds are outlined in black and white, and the leaflets within are of green

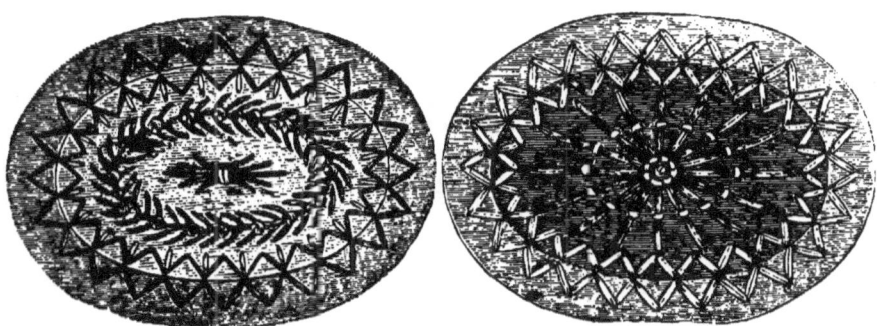

Fig. 28.—MEDALLION IN POINT RUSSE.   Fig. 29.—MEDALLION IN POINT RUSSE.

silk. The stars are outlined in black and blue, the crossings are red, and the dots yellow. The figure between the stars is black and yellow.

Fig. 30.—BORDER IN POINT RUSSE.

HERRING-BONE, OR FEATHER STITCH.

This is an old-fashioned embroidery stitch revived, which is always effective.

In ancient times, fine pieces of linen were embroidered all over with flower designs in outline, with here and there a portion filled in, and the stems worked in a close herring-bone stitch to give them strength and substance. Sometimes the whole design would be worked in this stitch, done so closely as to have the appearance of braid.

Some of this filled-in work was done in a peculiar manner from side to side. An oval leaf to be filled would be begun at the base with a few satin stitches, then when a point was reached where it was wide enough, instead of passing the thread all the way underneath to the opposite side, about one-third of the width of the leaf is taken up in the needle, and the next stitch is done in the same way on the opposite side of the leaf—working from side to side until the leaf becomes too narrow again, when it is finished with a few satin stitches.

This stitch throws all the silk to the top; and the crossing of the threads in the middle of the leaf has a very rich and soft effect—giving also the appearance of a vein.

Feather-stitch seems too well known to need description; and there is a great variety of it, from the simplest "herring-bone," to the prettiest feather-like vine; and it has the advantage of being very easily and quickly done.

It is merely button-hole stitch, in alternate loops and long stitches, sewed backwards. A design may be drawn first, if needed, to make the work regular; but with one straight pencil line as a guide, if the eye is not very correct, almost any one who can use a needle will be able to do feather-stitch.

This stitch is very much used in appliqué work; and it makes pretty dividing lines in ornamenting large articles.

We lately saw a table-cover worked entirely in feather-stitch, that had quite an Oriental appearance. The ground was black cloth; and all colors of worsted braid, of different widths, were sewed on with this stitch—being placed around an oblong piece in the centre, and in strips across to the edge for the border.

CHAIN-STITCH.

Another well-known and simple embroidery-stitch; and more beautiful effects may be produced with it than are known to the philosophy of the ordinary worker.

Chain-stitch is sometimes used for filled-in embroidery; the lines of the chain being laid very close together, and following the form of the leaf or flower until the space is filled. It should always be commenced on the outside, and worked to the centre.

Some very rich kinds of Algerian and Eastern work, often embroidered entirely with gold thread, and generally with a mixture of this with silk, are done altogether in chain-stitch. It is often found, too,

ARTISTIC EMBROIDERY. 29

Fig. 31.—Border for Furniture Covers, Portières, etc.—Chain Stitch Embroidery.

in ancient crewel-work; and is made by holding the thread firmly over the point of the needle, while it is drawn out, so as to form a loop. The needle is put back again into the centre of this loop; and the thread again passed over the point to form a second one—and so on, the succession of loops forming the chain.

The objection to this stitch is that it has a mechanical effect, and can be exactly imitated with the sewing-machine. The long embroidery-stitch is much more elastic and natural-looking, and able to accommodate itself better to varying forms. Chain-stitch is useful, however, for outline-work, and wherever a stronger line is required than that made by the long stitch.

Curtains, table-covers, portières, etc., are handsomely embroidered in chain-stitch; and Figure 31 gives a very rich bordering pattern for this purpose. Turkish embroidery is nearly always done in chain-stitch; and covers for small tables, with a light blue or scarlet ground, worked all over in chain-stitch arabesques with bright silks, make a pretty "bit of color" for a shaded corner.

Another effective way of working a table-cover in chain-stitch is to get black, red, and white cloth or flannel; the black for the centre, the red next to the black, and the white for the border—and joining them by lapping the edge of one a very little way over the other, proceed to chain-stitch the whole with various colored silks.

The effect is very handsome; and the bordering may differ from the other part by being done in loose overcast stitch over straight pieces of zephyr, and finished with little tassels of the bright silks.

Figure 32 is a very pretty Oriental-looking pattern suitable for a bordering, or it can be used in other ways. The figures placed

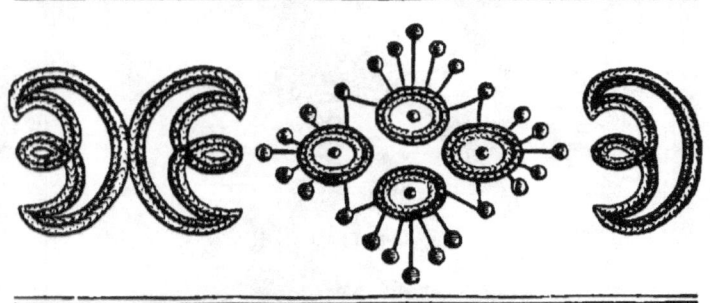

FIG. 32.—ORIENTAL BORDERING.

together are worked in chain-stitch with silk of two contrasting colors—two shades being used in each figure. The outer row of the first is dark-red, and the inner one bright-red. The second figure is of two shades of green; the third of two shades of blue; and the fourth of two shades of yellow. The knotted stitch in the centre of the ovals is violet. The dots outside the ovals are worked in satin-stitch, and are alternately red, yellow, violet, and blue. The stems are of black silk in point-russe stitches. The four ovals are worked in chain-stitch with silk of two shades of brown.

LADDER-STITCH.

This is sometimes quite effective in ornamental embroidery. Figures 33 and 34 give two different patterns. The material is partly cut away in these illustrations, and in some kinds of work this is a great improvement. Ladder-stitch makes very pretty border lines—the outer edges being done in overcast, and the cross-stitches in point-russe.

Fig. 33.

Fig. 34.

Exquisite pieces of work have been wrought in silk embroidery from time immemorial; and there is scarcely a material to which it may not be applied. A fragment of old embroidery, worked more than a century ago, is represented as a good subject for study in the way of coloring.

This fragment is about eight inches deep, intended for bordering, and is worked on white satin. The material is ravelled out in a fringe at the bottom; then comes a line about an eighth of an inch wide in dark red floss—then a row of disks shaded in a dark and a light green; above these and touching one another are two broader lines of red, one the same color as the first, the other paler; then there is a representation of moss worked in chenille of three shades of green—and from this mossy ground spring roses, carnations, forget-me-nots, and leafy sprays. This part is treated quite decoratively; and no attempt is made to preserve the natural proportions of the flowers in relation to each other, or to their stems and leaves.

In the sprays, one or two leaves are of peach-blossom color. Above this row of flowers are branches in festoons; of which the stems are olive-brown, the leaves shaded, or rather, party-colored, with peach-blossom inclining to pink, olive-brown, and two or three shades of green. It will be seen that nature is no more strictly adhered to in color than in form.

Over these branches is a pattern in two shades of peach-blossom, mingled with a very little blue. Except the moss, the embroidery is all done in floss silk split very fine. Seen by artificial light, this beautiful piece of work has the brilliancy of cut and polished gems; while the general effect of color is extremely rich and sweet, and would harmonize with almost any surroundings.

A beautiful way of treating the ground color, particularly if it be one that seems to attract too much attention to itself, is by working a small diaper pattern all over it in a darker shade of the same color —this gives depth and richness to the whole. A network of dead gold may be imitated in silk of the right shade.

Dark, brownish greens, deep, dull blues, and rich maroons, make good grounds; but black is best for a brilliant effect. The ground must be decidedly dark, or decidedly light—no half-way shades being allowable, as it is far more important for the colors of the work to contrast strongly with the ground than with each other.

CHINESE EMBROIDERY.

The French and Chinese excel in silk embroidery; and the painstaking double work done in China is well known. The great care with which the Chinese embroider preserves their materials bright and shining. These materials are floss and twisted silks—also the bark of a tree spun into a fine thread. Flat lines of gold also glitter among the silks, and are used as stems and connecting links.

The drawing of these embroideries is sometimes as uncouth as that of their paintings; but in some of their flowers (probably copied from nature) they are often even botanically correct. The iris, for instance, which frequently appears in their designs, is very true to nature; and so is the time-honored stork. The iris, Figure 35, is a good flower for embroidery; and may be made as effective in borders as the sunflower.

The modern art of embroidery in China is thus graphically described by a traveller:

"For 22 cash, or *tseen*, I purchased an elegant book filled with choice subjects of the graphic art as patterns for the use of the young needlewoman. She is assumed to be poor, and hence the little manual is printed at about one penny of our money. It has a cover of a fair yellow, studded with spangles of gold; and contains between two and three hundred figures culled from the various stores of nature and art.

"In fact, the objects are so well-selected and so numerous, that they might serve as illustrations to a small encyclopædia. One acquainted with Chinese literature and natural history might deliver several lectures with this book before him. The meadow, the grove, the brook, the antiquary's museum, and the pages of mythology, with the adornments of the house and garden, are all laid under contribution.

"The book is said to be for the use of the person who belongs to the *green window*—which is an epithet for the dwelling of a poor woman;

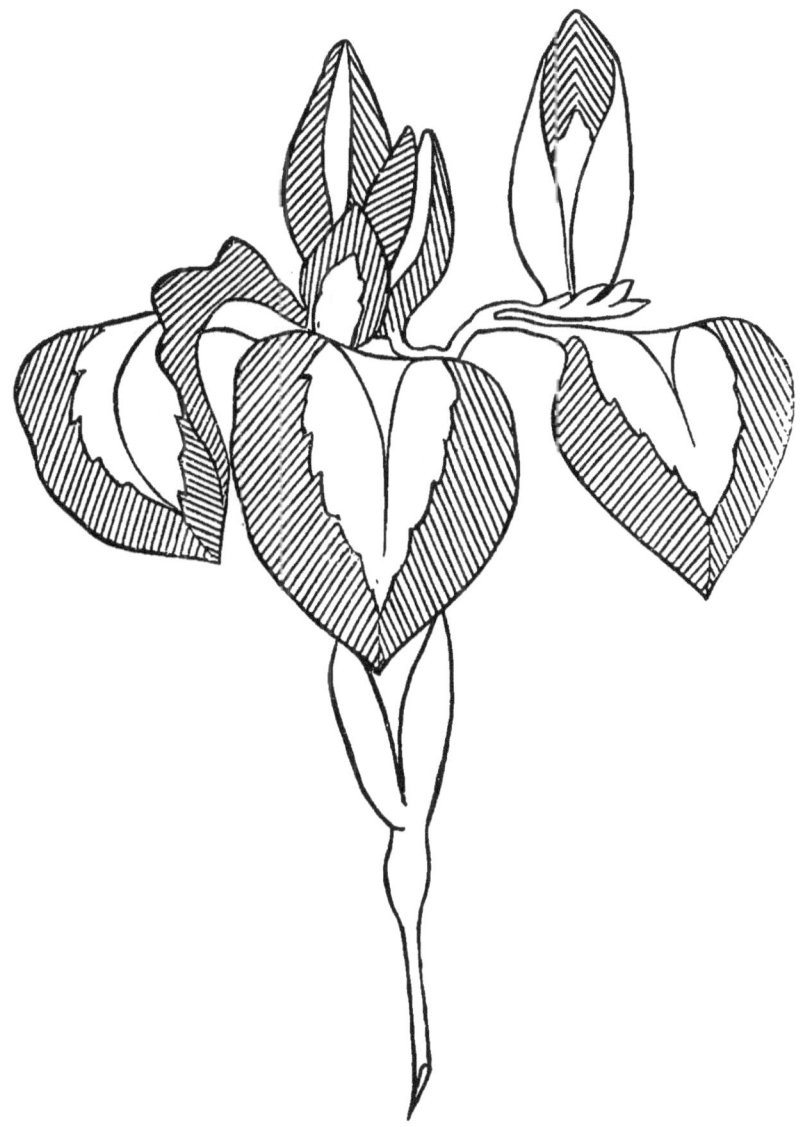

Fig. 35.

while the *red gallery* denotes the residence of a rich female. The industrious poor plies her task near the green lattice, which is made of earthenware and lets in both the light and the breath of heaven; while the rich dame leans upon the vermeil-tinted balusters of the gaudy veranda, and gazes carelessly at the sunbeams as they sparkle among the flowers, or waves the soft breeze which agitates the green roof of the Indian fig-tree.

"The title-page presents us with a venerable man in the weeds of office, holding in his hand a scroll with this motto: 'Heaven's Magistrate confers wealth.' Over his head are bats disporting among the clouds; the emblems, I suppose, of wakefulness—for these animals are on the alert while men sleep.

"I once saw two girls at this work in the village of Mongha. They were seated upon a low stool, and extended their legs across another of twice the height of their seat. In this way, a support was provided for the frame on which the piece to be embroidered was spread forth. Their faces wore a sickly hue; which was owing, perhaps, to close confinement and the unnatural position in which they were obliged to sit.

"The finest specimens of embroidery are, so far as my observation goes, done by men, who stand while at work—a practice which these damsels could not imitate, as their feet were small. They were poor, but too genteel, in their parents' idea, to do the drudgery of the humble housewife; and so their feet were bandaged and kept from growing beyond the limits of gentility. Their looks were not likely soon to attract a lover; and hence they were compelled to tease the sampler from the glistening dawn till dewy eve."

Chinese embroidery is particularly rich and effective for screens, with its clear outlines, its gorgeous flowers, and showy birds and butterflies. It bears the closest scrutiny—each stitch, even the hair lines, seems to be placed just in the right spot; and appliqué is often brought in so successfully, that it looks as if woven in the material. The vivid clusters of crêpe flowers are beautiful; and the judicious introduction of gold thread here and there gives a marvellous richness to the whole work.

Very fine floss-silk is the most common material used, and the embroidery is done in long irregular stitches. Silk and satin are generally used for the foundation; but whether the color is vivid blue, bright scarlet, or pale gold, the effect seems to be equally good.

The apparent carelessness of this work is one of its great attractions; the bold, free outlines seem easy of imitation; and a study of the cheap Chinese and Japanese fans will be found very suggestive in the way of design and coloring. A simple design on one of these fans has an intensely blue sky at the upper edge—a white moon in its first quarter at the upper right-hand corner—while at the left-hand lower one, a small bunch of intensely pink flowers send a warm glow over the whole. The effect is extremely pretty.

Japanese embroidery, although similar in style and design, seems finer and more dainty than the Chinese; and yet it is said that their best specimens of work are kept for home decoration. The finest of these are the cloths used as covers for the presents given by persons paying visits of ceremony; these cloths are not given with the presents they cover, but are family heirlooms. Really good Japanese work is said to be rarely seen elsewhere.

The pieces of embroidery which are done purposely for a foreign market are often very handsome; but they do not compare with those which are executed for their own critical eyes. White birds, usually storks, on a black satin ground, from which they stand out so clearly that they seem in the very act of flying, are the most common subject. Some rare pieces are occasionally seen in which the work is exquisite; in one, the ground will be a deep, soft blue satin, like the sky of a summer night; while the leading colors of the embroidery are gold, pale blue, and white.

In another piece, the ground is of scarlet moreen, of a sufficiently bright yellow scarlet to harmonize with the gold that forms the principal color in the embroidery. The subject is a long flight of storks; not less than eighty of them are flying upwards in a zigzag line—the angles of which are very carefully studied from the bottom to the top of the picture.

Most of these storks are embroidered in white silk, the direction of the stitches giving much of their form; they are pricked out with black, and there is a little pale pink or pale yellow-green in their beaks and legs. About a quarter of them are worked all in gold—representing the birds in shadow, or seen against the light; and these have little or no detail. Each bird is distinct, separately drawn, and having his own expression, mode of flight, and position in the line.

The rest of the space is filled by horizontal bars of gold of varying widths, and groups of fan-stitches also in gold; these seem to indicate the flat sunset clouds and the tops of the distant trees passed over by the storks in their flight.

Both in Japanese and Chinese work, the subjects are sometimes partly painted and partly embroidered; and the two are so happily blended, that it is difficult, at a little distance, to see where one kind of work stops and the other begins.

In imitating this kind of embroidery for small articles, unmeaning kinds of lines in the way of reeds and grasses, as in Figure 36, have a particularly characteristic look. Small fans may also be introduced to advantage; and Figure 37 would admit of a small bird and bough at the top on a gold-colored ground, with brown lines for sticks; while Figure 38 might have a top of pink floss or embroidery silk with

36　ARTISTIC EMBROIDERY.

black lines at the bottom. These fans may be very much varied, and can be made extremely ornamental. Figure 39 is a still different shape.

Fig. 36.

A full-sized fan with small ones embroidered over it would be a pretty conceit; or to introduce them in connection with flowers, butterflies, and other emblems of summer.

It must be borne in mind that this kind of work is never overloaded—a few grasses, a butterfly, and a flower, often sufficing for a good-sized object.

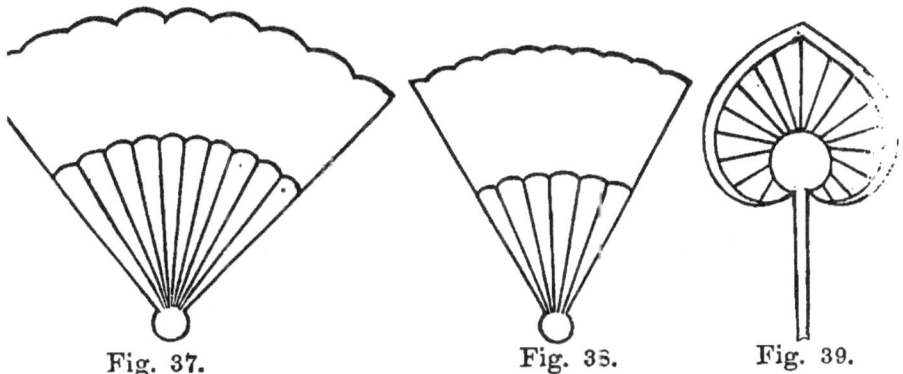

Fig. 37.　　　　　　Fig. 38.　　　　Fig. 39.

CHAPTER IV.

DESIGNING AND TRANSFERRING DESIGNS.

This is a most important part of the work, and one that is done in various ways. Patterns can always be stamped at the various fancy-work stores, or bought all ready for working; but the embroiderer, with original ideas and some turn for drawing, prefers to do this herself.

Worsted patterns may often be used for outlines, as they are generally correct in this respect, and the leaves particularly are well drawn. But those who are able to take their models from nature will have less stiffness in their work; and a little practice in this way will sometimes develop powers hitherto undreamed of. Large single flowers of all kinds are easiest to begin with; and a lily, or a wild rose, for instance, will be found quite easy to manage.

A pencil-drawing or a water-color painting can often be accommodated to embroidery; and a too spreading branch or cluster may be made more compact by a little management. A spray of apple-blossoms, which is a particularly desirable model, will frequently overstep the bounds assigned to it in one way, and not sufficiently fill them up in another. The best way to manage is to take a piece of paper the size of the article to be embroidered, and divide it by lines into four equal parts. The outline of the branch can then be sketched on it; and the result will probably be that two of the squares are filled, one barely touched with a leaf, and the other quite empty. More blossoms, leaves, or twigs, can be added on one side and taken away on the other; if the whole ground is not sufficiently covered, a butterfly, or a bird, may be introduced to furnish a bare corner.

The suitableness of any design for the purpose to which it is to be applied depends upon whether its position is to be a horizontal or an upright one.

Borders of upright sprigs, intended for a horizontal position, single or grouped, require a line or two below, which serves to keep them together; without this support they look disjointed, and each sprig is too independent of the others. They need not touch the line—but one near at hand seems to keep them from falling into space. When the sprigs are large a series of lines should be used; and for this purpose very pretty designs are often found in Oriental china.

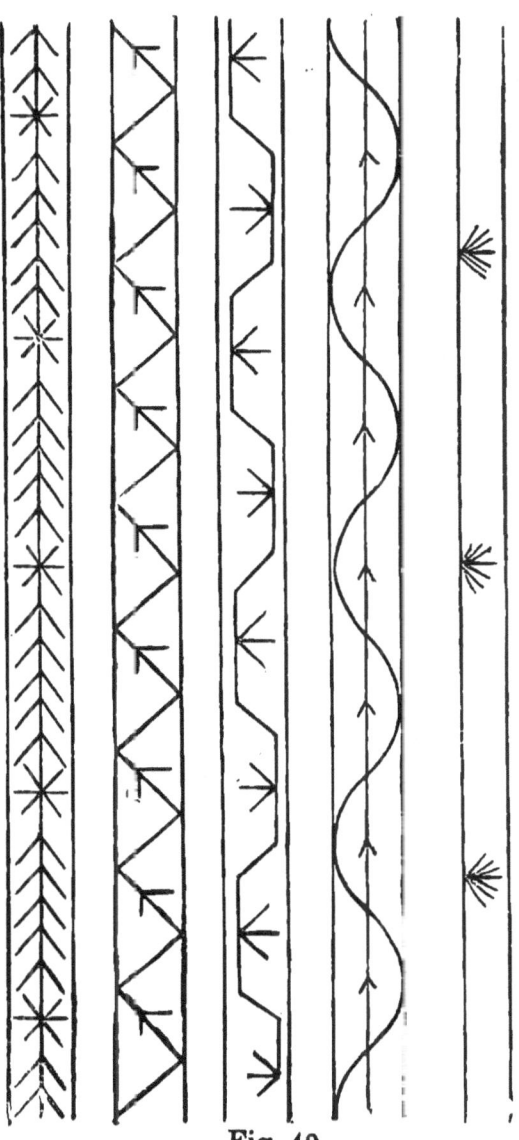

Fig. 40.

The combination in Figure 40 is simple enough in detail, but very effective to edge a bordering. It is done in chain-stitch, ladder-stitch, and point russe.

Small borders are often improved by a mere line on each side; and the same effect is produced by sewing the bordering on material of a different shade.

Birds and butterflies are naturally associated with flowers; they give an air of life, and often serve to balance the inequalities of a design. Butterflies are particularly appropriate from their great variety both of size and coloring; and being worked like other artistic embroidery, without any elaboration of detail, they are very easily done.

Vases, which frequently occur in the fashionable designs, should either be represented by some material laid on, or worked in lines only—the outline with the pattern on it, as it would appear in a pencil drawing without shading.

A beautiful piece of silk embroidery was worked on a ground of bronze-green satin. There were sprays of convolvulus springing from a vase of gray satin; the flowers were white, edged with pure blue—not the purplish blue of the natural flower, for that would not have harmonized so well—and yet there was nothing unnatural in the effect of the color. The leaves were of yellow and gray greens, and the stalks a brownish green.

Then, to give warmth and life, some sulphur butterflies hovered over the garlands. Thus, though in the coloring of the design the component parts only of the bronze-green ground were used, the effect was perfect.

TRANSFERRING DESIGNS.

Designs are traced in various ways, according to the nature and color of the material to be embroidered.

For a light-colored ground, the best method is to trace the pattern on tissue or other thin paper, lay the material flat upon a table, and fix the place of the pattern upon it very exactly. Then put a piece of carbonized blue or black paper, face downward, on the material, between it and the paper pattern; and with a stiletto, or other hard-pointed but not too sharp instrument (a metallic pencil or a knitting-needle will often answer the purpose), trace over all the lines of the design, taking care to keep the paper pattern from slipping, and that the fingers do not press too heavily on the transferring-paper, or more color will come off than is desirable.

An *old* sheet of paper is more satisfactory than a new one; and it is advisable to rub the latter gently with a cloth before using it, to remove any unfixed coloring.

Pouncing is a more complicated process than tracing; but for dark-colored materials it is safer.

The design must first be drawn on thick paper, and then pricked along the lines with a pin. The paper should then be held up to the light to see that the holes are clear, and close enough together to make the pattern plain.

When the pattern is fixed, face upward, on the material, dust it over with starch tied up in thin muslin so that the fine powder goes through the holes. Flour will answer the purpose, and may be best applied about the pattern with a soft brush.

The paper must then be taken up very carefully, lifting it straight upward off the material so that it does not blur the little dots of white, which ought to be in regular order underneath—marking out the design. The lines of the pattern should be traced at once, as indicated by the dots, with the original design before the eye, with white tracing paint.

There is also a *blue* powder for delicate light materials, that might be injured by the carbonized paper.

Another method, when the nature of the design will permit it, is to cut out the pattern in paper, place it on the material, and trace round the edges with chalk. Then remove the paper, and go over the chalk outline with Chinese white—renewing it where it is defective.

The richer the fabric, the more care, of course, is needed in transferring the design; and transparent materials should have the pattern basted underneath. Embroidery in floss is often done on black net—for which the design should be managed in this way.

CHAPTER V.

ARTICLES IN SILK EMBROIDERY.

There is scarcely an article for which ornament of this kind is used that may not be decorated with silk embroidery, and it is suitable for all materials. Curtains, portières, and table-covers are very handsome done in outline with silk of the same color, but a lighter shade than the ground; and whole sets of furniture have been undertaken by ambitious workers.

A SCREEN OF PEACOCK FEATHERS.

This was embroidered on a foundation of pale peach-blossom silk with split floss, and made up with a plain ebony frame, ornamented here and there with a little dead gold.

It was an exquisite piece of work, both in design and execution; and so wonderfully did the brilliant silks reflect the changeful hues of the bronze-greens and browns, that it was difficult to convince visitors that real feathers were not fastened on. The only pattern used by the embroiderer was one tail-feather dropped by a majestic fowl almost at her feet; and while walking with the trophy in her hand, the design of the screen came to her and was forthwith executed.

It was a good-sized fire-place screen; and as the room was furnished in dark-blue, it showed to great advantage.

A PRETTY BANNER-SCREEN.

This was fastened to the end of the mantel; and the crimson satin foundation was covered with a small diaper pattern in maroon silk. Thick clusters of small daisies without leaves were worked as a bordering in embroidery-stitch; the centres in knot-stitch. In the middle of the screen was a beautifully-designed monogram in gold-colored silk.

ANOTHER BANNER-SCREEN

was attached to a gilt stand. This stood on a table and was intended to shade the eyes from a lamp or candle. The ground was of pale green silk, and it was beautifully embroidered with ivy-leaves of darker shades. In the centre, there was an antique lamp done in gold thread; and the banner was finished with a chenille fringe of green and white. It was lined with white silk.

EMBROIDERED TABLE-TOP.

Figure 41 may be used for a variety of purposes. It makes a very pretty top for a small table; and is worked in stalk-stitch, chain-stitch, point russe, and knotted stitch, with the flowers in pink, claret-color, and yellow, on a pale-blue ground. The sprays and leaves are in shades of olive-green.

The table, which looks best with a pedestal of ebony, or ebonized wood, has a border-fringe of Macramé lace.

WINDOW-CURTAIN BORDER.

A very handsome bordering for window-curtains was lately worked by an artistic needle-woman; figures of dragons in gold-colored embroidery-silk on a ground of maroon rep. The bordering was intended for a soft gray material; and the straight cornice-band was embroidered in the same device.

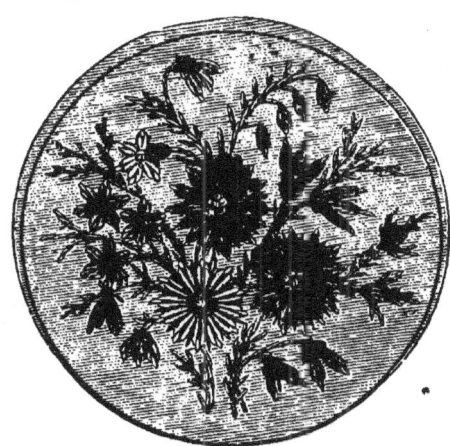

Fig. 41.

EMBROIDERED DRESSES.

Silk embroidery is very ornamental for dresses—although for this purpose usually done only in one color. Ordinarily, it would be a formidable piece of work to do it in the style of smaller articles; but ingenuity and rapid execution sometimes go hand in hand. The heroine of a story is represented as threading her needle with one length of crimson silk, and with this scanty material, bringing out a crimson rose on a silk handkerchief almost as quickly as a magician could do it. A few deft stitches—and there it was. It was taken to pieces quite as easily, and no trace of it remained.

But embroidery does not usually go on in this fashion; it is careful work; and she who takes the greatest pains, as a general thing meets with the best success.

Embroidered robes for full dress are decidedly the fashion now; and one of black silk, or lace, embroidered with carnations, is beautiful for a brunette—while the delicate blonde may wreathe herself with blue convolvulus, or deeply-pink wild roses, on a white or cream-colored ground. Every one has her favorite flower; and to wear it embroidered on an evening dress is a graceful way of proclaiming it.

PANELS.

Painted panels and tiles have become almost a mania; but the needle of the embroideress can produce quite as charming results. Painting is more quickly done; but every one cannot paint, while many who cannot do this can embroider exquisitely.

To keep the embroidered panel or tile fresh and bright, it should be protected by glass; and properly treated, it will be quite as satisfactory as painting.

The two panels for the doors of a small hanging-cabinet are very pretty with a ground of cloth-of-gold, gold-colored satin, or silk—a spray of wistaria worked on one—wild roses on the other. Violets and anemones are pretty together; and on anything with four panels may be represented the flowers or birds of the four seasons.

Silhouettes in black silk may be worked on all colored grounds for tiles; and ingenuity can accomplish wonders in this way. The whole procession of flowers, from the first snow-drop, or hepatica, of early spring, to the holly and berries of Christmas, may be followed up on tiles; the fans and umbrellas of all nations; and various other suggestions, both practical and amusing.

SMALL CURTAINS OR HANGINGS

For cabinets and book-shelves may be made of various materials, and ornamented with silk embroidery. The patterns should be more delicate and finished, and the materials of finer quality than for large hangings. Arabesques of chain-stitch in gold-colored silk on a dark-blue ground of velveteen, with a pretty border pattern at top and bottom; or a bright-colored bird on a branch, with a butterfly in one corner, for a back-ground; buttercups and daisies on a ground of golden-brown, would all be effective.

A WREATHED PICTURE.

Something new in the way of embroidery is to border a picture in this manner. The frames with painted corners may be imitated with the needle, and the daisies, violets, and other flowers will be found quite as ornamental in embroidery.

But the wreathed picture was a fine engraving of the Mater Dolorosa, small enough to make the process practicable. It was unmounted, and the back carefully pasted on the foundation of light-blue satin. Not a wrinkle was visible after it was thoroughly smoothed with a soft piece of old cambric; and after sewing a piece of narrow, gold-colored silk braid around the edge, a wreath of Annunciation lilies was traced and embroidered on the satin. It was so beautifully done as to look like painting; and with a glass over the whole the illusion was complete. It was put in a gilded Florentine frame.

AN EMBROIDERED ROOM.

It was very pretty to read about in a story, and not impossible to carry out practically. The prevailing colors of the room were pale-blue and carnation; and the curtain-lambrequins of pale-blue were embroidered with sprays of woodbine in its autumn dress of vivid scarlet and crimson. The mantel-hanging was in blocks like tiles, done in the same colors; and the panels of a home-made cabinet were likewise embroidered.

These things, with other accessions, made it a charming room; and if one could walk bodily into just such an apartment, the effect would doubtless be all that it was represented.

A FAN TABLE-COVER.

Outlined palm leaves are very pretty, and fans are no less so. The groundwork of cloth, flannel, or satin (if a small table), has three or five parallel strips of velvet ribbon sewn down on each side with point russe stitches of gold-colored silk, and put far enough apart for fans of all colors to be embroidered between them.

These are worked in long embroidery-stitch; and although less work if merely outlined, they are so very much richer and brighter looking when filled in as to be quite worth the trouble. The ground may be of any color that harmonizes with the rest of the room.

A CHAIR-COVER.

Long embroidered strips that will cover both back and seat of the kind of lounging-chair now so much in use are very pretty worked like the table-cover—the groundwork of the middle strip being of gray satin or velveteen, with the rows of fans separated by garnet-colored velvet ribbon, and a strip of the same colored velveteen on either side of the gray. A fringe where the covering ends at top and bottom gives it the look of being carelessly thrown there.

FIRE-SCREENS.

We have just been shown two exquisite pieces of embroidery intended for fire-screens. One represented flame-colored gladioli on a black satin ground, and was rich beyond expression; the other was worked with cat-tails, reeds, and some unpretending little yellow flowers on a blue ground. The material looked like a Chinese groundwork.

The coloring of both of these needle-paintings was perfect; and as to the stitches, it was difficult to believe that there were any—the shades were blended as if with a brush.

A CHILD'S AFGHAN.

It was made of strips of pink and white cashmere; the pink ones embroidered with daisies, the white ones with pansies, in embroidery-silk—and it was one of the prettiest things of the kind ever seen. It was lined with thin pink silk slightly wadded and quilted, and bordered with a ruching of pink ribbon. The seams were concealed by lines of feather-stitch in garnet-colored silk.

The resources of silk embroidery are inexhaustible; and all sorts of small articles, pin-cushions, brackets, watch-stands, glove-boxes, sachets, etc., will suggest themselves. Fans, too, are beautifully embroidered, and divide admiration with fine painting. Ornamental velvets for neck, wrists, and belt, are a fashionable device—and these are embroidered with single flowers: daisies, violets, etc.

CHAPTER VI.

PRINT-WORK.

This is a very fine kind of embroidery, and specimens of it are quite rare. As the name implies, it is intended to imitate a picture, and is generally used only for small subjects—the stitches being almost too minute to be distinguished at all.

It is done on white silk or satin, which is carefully stretched in a frame, and the design is then drawn on it. This is sketched with a pencil, and usually worked in black silk; the various shades between black and white may be used, but not colors—as the object is to represent an engraving. Lead color, or pale slate, will be as suitable as black.

A very fine needle must be used, and fine silk to correspond; and a dotted engraving can be so well imitated in this kind of work that it is almost impossible to tell the difference. The stitch used is known as masking-stitch; and it is set as closely as possible without lapping one over another.

In working a copy of an engraving, the embroiderer begins with the darkest shades, which are done with black silk; gradually proceeding to the lightest tints, with silks of the intermediate shades—blending them into each other with the nicest care. To accomplish this, where it is necessary to introduce the lighter portions, the stitches are set wide apart and the intervals filled up by putting in the lightest tint used.

The worker must always have the engraving before her to study the lights and shades. Fine engravings can be copied in the same way—but the stitches should be longer and wider apart.

This kind of needlework requires great patience and is a heavy strain upon the eyesight; and considering the beautiful effects produced by other methods with less outlay, it is not likely to become very popular.

CHAPTER VII.

SILK EMBROIDERY WITH GOLD.

Much of the ancient work used for hangings was magnificently wrought with a mixture of gold embroidery—as much of the Indian needlework is now done, especially in Japan and China. The royal palace of Jeddo has a profusion of the finest tapestry, wrought by the most curious hands, and adorned with pearls, gold, and silver, and other costly embellishments.

The Moors of Spain have been especially celebrated for their rich and beautiful decorative work; and with them originated the custom of using tapestry for curtains. Mohammed forbade his followers to imitate animals, or insects, in their ornamental work; and from this circumstance, the term Arabesque, which represents their style of decoration, was used to express all odd combinations of patterns from which human and animal forms were excluded.

Gold was introduced into these arabesques with the richest possible effect; and this style of design has never lost its popularity. It is often mixed with other patterns in colors; but the simple richness of an arabesque in black and gold cannot be excelled.

In the Middle Ages the most beautiful gold embroidery was called *opus Anglicanum;* and this name clung to it whether it was done in England or not. Much of this work was done in the convents, or "shee-schools," as quaint old Fuller calls them; and besides church vestments, which will be mentioned elsewhere, very beautiful secular robes and pieces of tapestry were wrought in silk and gold.

The richest tapestry was in pieces like large flags or banners; and was a prominent decoration on all occasions of festivity or rejoicing. Ornamental needlework of all kinds was hung from the windows, or balconies, in those streets through which a pageant, or festal procession, was to pass—just as flags are suspended now; and as the houses were then built with the upper stories far overhanging the lower ones, these draperies frequently hung in rich folds to the ground. When a street was thus adorned through its whole length, and partly roofed by the floating streamers and banners above, it must have had somewhat the appearance of a suite of magnificent saloons.

The art of embroidering with gold and silver is very ancient, and these costly materials were often woven into fabrics as well; but the pure metal was then used, beaten into thin plates, and then cut into narrow slips, which were rounded with a hammer and filed to make threads or wire.

The method is exactly described in Exodus xxxix. 3, as practised by the Israelites: "And they did beat the gold into thin plates, and cut it into wires, to work it in the blue, and in the purple, and in the scarlet, and in the fine linen with cunning work."

Old embroidered robes are mentioned made entirely of these gold threads without any linen or woolen ground. Pieces of embroidery worked with gold were called "orphreys," from the mediæval *aurifrigium* or *aurifrasium;* and mention is made, in the reign of Edward III., of two vests of green velvet embroidered with gold, one of which was decorated with sea-sirens bearing a shield with the arms of England and Hainault. Also of a robe of velvet worked with gold; and an outer garment wrought with pelicans, images, and tabernacles of gold.

An ancient Persian carpet was of silk and cloth of gold sixty cubits square. It was intended to represent a garden; and the figures were of gold embroidery, with the colors heightened by precious stones; the ruby, the sapphire, the beryl, the topaz, and the pearl, being arranged with great skill to represent, in beautiful mosaic, trees, fruit and flowers, rivulets, fountains, and shrubs of every description.

These specimens, however, are things of the past.

MODERN WORK

of this kind is generally used in large and bold designs, where much display and extreme brilliancy are desired.

In these days, instead of the pure metal, silver, or copper wire, gilt is used. Silver threads are covered either with the pure metal, or with plated copper. The Chinese very cunningly use slips of gilt paper which they twist upon silk threads, and with which they manage to produce very beautiful effects.

MATERIALS USED.

Cord, braid, thread, bullion, spangles, beads, passing, etc., are all used in gold embroidery, and in embroidery with gold and silk.

Of these, "passing," as it is termed, is the finest material of the kind. It is a smooth thread of an even size, and resembles a thin, metallic wire—differing from gold cord in the closeness with which the flattened wire is spirally twisted round the silk, and in being formed of only one thread.

It is used in the same way as silk, the stitch being generally satin-stitch; and the needle should be an ordinary needle with a large eye, and coarse enough to prevent the fretting of the gold as it is passed backwards and forwards through the work.

Beautiful embroidery is wrought by the Turks with "passing" on Morocco.

GOLD CORD.

This is a twist of two or more threads, which are wound around with the flattened wires in a contrary direction to that of "passing"—two, three, or four threads being used for needlework.

Cord is often employed for edging braid-work, or flat embroidery—also for working braiding-patterns. It is also used with beautiful effect as a ground for small, ornamental articles. Fine silk of the same color is best for sewing it on; and great care must be taken, in doing this, not to chip the metal surface, or the silk will show beneath and give the work a broken appearance. The needle should be held as horizontally as possible, and passed between the interstices of the cord—slightly catching up a thread or two of the material it is intended to ornament.

GOLD BRAID.

This is a kind of plaited lace, made of three or more threads. There are various qualities and makes, suited to different purposes, and great judgment is required in their selection. When it is to be used on velvet, a round, full, close make should be chosen.

It may be bought of various widths; and as a general thing, the less gold there is about it, the cheaper it is, and the more liable to tarnish. Mosaic, or copper-gilt, is the least expensive, and also the least durable.

BULLION.

This is a very rich and effective material—being made of a fine wire so exquisitely twisted, that it forms a smooth, round, elastic tube, which may be cut with scissors into the necessary lengths.

There are three kinds of bullion: rough, smooth, and checked—all of which are frequently used together in the same piece of work. When a large letter, for instance, is to be embroidered in bullion, after it is traced, the surface is raised with cotton, and the bullion cut into pieces of the proper size; then three stitches might be made with the smooth, two with the rough, and two with the checked; then, again, two with the rough and three with the smooth; this would form a kind of pattern, and add very much to the richness of the letter.

Short pieces of bullion can be introduced into patterns worked with gold thread to great advantage—two or three of them in the cup of a flower, and in various other ways. To fasten them on properly, take the stitch (the needle being threaded with gold-colored silk) lengthwise of the bullion, through the twist—this causes it to lie flat on the foundation.

Stars of every form may be made in this way: they are extremely brilliant. The centres of flowers are often formed of bullion; in that case, however, the stitch does not pass through the twist its full length, but is shorter—so that the middle of the bullion is depressed, and the extremities elevated; or the stitch may be passed through both ends of the piece of bullion, and being drawn rather tight, a slight prominence, or expansion, will be given to the middle. Either method has a beautiful effect.

SPANGLES.

These are small pieces of silver or other metal, gilt or plated—cut into various forms, though usually round—and with a hole in the centre through which the silk is passed that fastens them to the work. It is not easy to secure them properly, and at the same time to conceal the means by which it is done. The only way to accomplish it is to bring the silk from the under side and pass it through the small hole in the centre of the spangle; the needle is next to be passed through a very small piece of bullion, and then put back through the hole again. This does away with the unsightly appearance of a thread across the spangle, and makes it more secure.

Spangles were once extensively used in decorative work, to give it richness and glitter; but now they are chiefly used to ornament fringes and tassels, and other Masonic paraphernalia. Their value depends on their brillianey and color, and the amount of gold used in their gilding.

Spangled fans are very showy; and black satin or black tulle is a good foundation for showing them to advantage.

GOLD THREAD.

This belongs more particularly, perhaps, to "the art of sewing in golde and silke;" and "a robe of Indian silk thickly wrought with flowers of gold" was certainly a gorgeous object. Another robe was adorned with roses of gold wrought with marvellous skill, and bordered with pearls and precious stones of exceeding value.

Various materials are used as foundations for embroidery in gold thread: crape, India muslin, or some kind of silk, being usually preferred as giving the best effect, and displaying the rich devices to the greatest advantage.

The thread used should be fine and even in texture; a little care in this matter will make the work comparatively easy. Satin-stitch is the one generally used; and if the material to be embroidered is transparent, the pattern is laid *under* the foundation, and the outline traced in white thread.

In working a slender flower-stalk, the running thread of white should be omitted; gold thread should be run in, and then slightly sewed over with another thread of gold; this will give a spiral appearance, which is very beautiful.

In using silk with gold thread, it is best to use silk of one color—a variety of colors tending to destroy the harmony of contrast. Green and gold have always been close friends, and silk of a bright green mingled with the gold thread has a very rich effect. Gray and gold, black and gold, and many other combinations might be mentioned; but a green branch or sprigs embroidered in silk, with flowers formed of gold thread and bullion, is as pretty a one as can be made.

In working crests, however, or coats-of-arms, in which gold thread is much used, the heraldic arrangement of metals and colors must be faithfully followed. In such cases, the silk must be of as many colors as in the arms when properly emblazoned; and great care must be taken in working devices in imitation of arms, never to place a metal upon a metal, or a color upon a color.

In some very rich Indian work lately seen, the ground was of gold thread worked in spirals—the rich colors of embroidery silks laid on this made it perfectly dazzling.

India muslins are sometimes worked with a gilt or plated sheet of very thin metal cut into strips, or any shape wanted, with scissors. Tinsel is an imitation of it, and it comes in various colors.

Gold beads and gold and silver fringes are more or less used. These all vary greatly in size and quality, and are valuable according to the amount of gold used in their manufacture.

Silver thread, cord, or braid, is more likely to tarnish than gold, and is not so rich-looking. There is, besides, embroidery silk of a decidedly silver white, which produces almost the effect of silver thread or cord.

CHAPTER VIII.

EMBROIDERED BOOKS AND OTHER ARTICLES.

> "And often did she look
> On that which in her hand she bore,
> In velvet bound and broidered o'er—
> Her breviary book."
>
> MARMION.

WHEN books were regarded as precious treasures, and the purchase of a single volume involved as much outlay as a rare painting, before the art of printing became established, the caskets that held such valuable possessions were deemed worthy of much labor and expense.

Rare old carved ivory, gold and silver plates, and precious stones, were often used on book-covers; and the most ancient existing specimen of this gorgeous style of book-making is written in silver and gold letters on a purple ground. Rich and curious devices were often wrought with the needle on the velvet, or brocade, which last became more exclusively the fashionable material for binding.

The new passion for books which was at its height in Queen Elizabeth's day made the ornamentation of book-covers a favorite employment of the high-born dames of England. A book of rhetoric of that time has been preserved as much for the sake of the outside as for its contents. The cover is of crimson satin, on which is embroidered a coat-of-arms: a lion rampant in gold thread on a blue field, with a transverse badge in scarlet silk, the minor ornaments all wrought in fine gold thread.

A MAROON-VELVET BOOK.

Another old book is bound in rich maroon velvet, with the royal arms, the garter and motto embroidered in blue; on a ground of crimson, the *fleur-de-lys*, leopards, and letters of the motto are worked in gold thread. A coronet, or crown of gold, is inwrought with pearls; at the corners are roses in red silk and gold; the cover is finished with a narrow border in burnished gold thread.

A QUEEN'S NEEDLEWORK.

A book of prayers copied out by Queen Elizabeth before she

54   ARTISTIC EMBROIDERY.

ascended the throne is covered with canvas wrought all over, in a kind of tent-stitch, with rich crimson silk and silver thread intermixed.

Fig. 42.—Border for Cover of Bible, Prayer-Book, etc.

Elizabeth's own needle worked the ornaments, consisting of the letters "H. K.," intertwined in the middle—a smaller "K" above and below—and roses in the corners—all very much raised, and worked in blue silk and silver.

PETRARCH'S SONNETS.

An edition of Petrarch's Sonnets, printed at Venice in 1544, is still in beautiful preservation. The back is of dark crimson velvet; and on each side is worked a large royal coat-of-arms in silk and gold highly raised. The book belonged to Edward VI.

ANOTHER ROYAL BOOK

has a cover of crimson silk with a Prince's feather worked in gold thread in the centre. The three feathers are bound together with large pearls and wreathed with leaves and flowers. Round the edge of the cover there is a broader wreath; and corner-sprigs in gold thread are thickly interspersed with spangles and gold leaves.

These elegant volumes,

> "In velvet bound and broidered o'er,"

are to be seen in the British Museum; and although the day is past for adorning book-covers in so showy a fashion, these articles may be more modestly ornamented with very good effect.

Kid, or leather, makes a very suitable cover for a Bible or Prayer-Book. Two shades of brown may be used for the border pattern in Figure 42—the figures in the lighter shade to be worked around with gold thread, either in chain-stitch or in stalk-stitch. Silk may be substituted for the gold thread.

A ground of gray kid, with the figures in black edged with gold, would be equally suitable. On one side of the cover, a small cross to match the border—and on the other, the owner's monogram would make an appropriate finish for either book.

The rich design in Figure 43 is on a foundation of black velvet, to which white faille is applied around the cross.

The figures of the design being outlined, the lines are run on the edges with maize-colored silk—going back and forth, and overcasting them with gold bullion. The passion-flowers, wheat, leaves, and ornaments of the cross, are worked in satin-stitch with gold thread. For the stems and vines, gold cord is sewed on with gold-colored silk.

A BOOK OF ENGRAVINGS

would be very ornamental with an embroidered cover. Crimson or maroon-colored velveteen, brown kid, or gray canvas, could be handsomely worked with silk and gold thread. Bordering of catalogues and circulars might be copied to advantage—some of

Fig. 43.—Cover for Prayer-Book.

these being very rich: black, with gold bars and dots, pink, crimson, or blue.

ARTISTIC EMBROIDERY. 57

Heraldic devices, rich monograms, dainty corners, all look well in this kind of work; and a bordering of gold acorns, or clover leaves, on a brown or olive ground, is always handsome.

SCRAP-BOOK COVERS.

may be made as attractive as the contents, according to the style of the illustrations. Russia duck is a very good foundation; and if the contents are of a comic nature, a Chinese or Japanese figure, or dragon, or either uncanny beast or bird, may be outlined and made very rich and showy with embroidery in the proper colors mixed with gold thread or braid.

Pongee, too, may be nicely embroidered; and is very pretty for thin books tied with a ribbon at the back. In this way, the contents can be changed at pleasure.

ALBUM COVERS

should be more delicate, and worked on velvet, or silk. Figure 44 makes a very pretty corner for this purpose; and Figure 45 is very effective

Fig. 44.—CORNER OF BORDER IN SATIN STITCH EMBROIDERY FOR ALBUM COVERS, PORTFOLIOS, ETC.

on a small book. The stars might be done in gold thread, the centre in point-russe with black silk—the diamonds in satin-stitch of a lighter or darker shade of the same color as the foundation.

Portfolios may be embroidered in the same way; and whether for writing materials or for engravings, they can be made very ornamental.

LETTER-CASE.

A very rich and handsome letter-case is represented in Figures 46 and 47: Figure 46 showing it when completed, and Figure 47 displaying the principal part of the embroidery.

The most suitable ground for the rich gold embroidery is velvet-

Fig. 45.

brown, crimson, or blue; but it may be made very handsomely in kid or morocco. The larger part of the case is eleven inches long, and eight inches wide; on the upper part of this book, there is a pattern in gold soutache, and the word LETTERS or LETTRES embroidered in gold bullion; beneath this, there is a pattern worked with white satin beads, edged round with fine white chenille—the scroll pattern is embroidered in gold.

The second part is placed over the lower part of the first, and forms the pocket which holds the letters. The central flower is formed with

Fig. 46.

eleven oval beads, edged with white chenille; another white bead is placed in the centre, and edged with gold. The other flowers are also composed of white satin beads edged with gold.

ARTISTIC EMBROIDERY.

GOLD AND SILK EMBROIDERY.

This rich pattern is intended for a cushion, or chair-cover. It is particularly handsome on a ground of blue velvet, or satin; and the

Fig. 47.

large flowers, leaves, and stems, are all outlined with gold thread sewed on with fine yellow silk. The stamens are worked in satin-

Fig. 48.

stitch with yellow silk, and the veins in point-russe with blue silk.

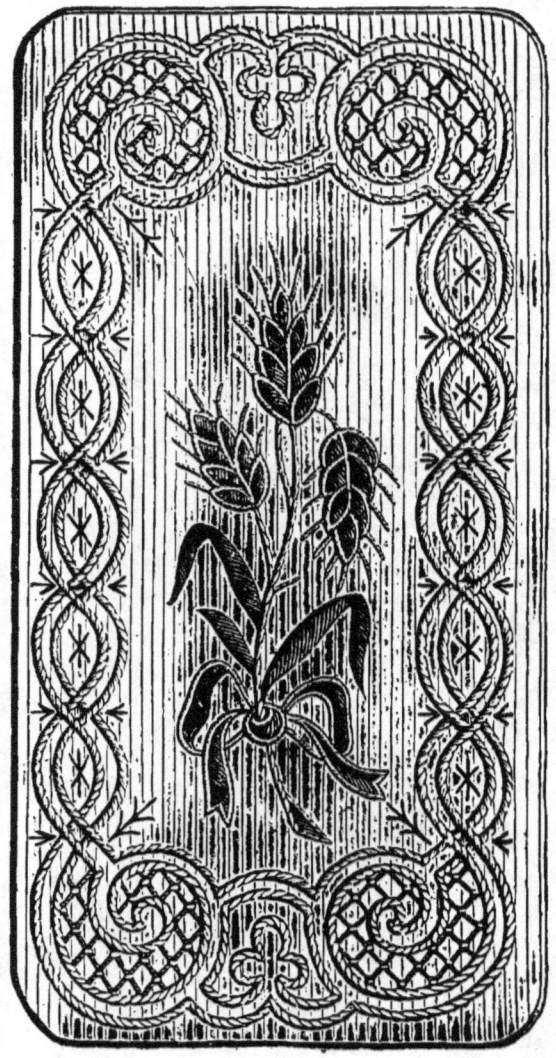

Fig. 49.

The forget-me-nots are done in satin-stitch with blue silk, and the centres in knotted-stitch with gold thread. The veins and stems are done in stalk-stitch, and the sprays and vines in point-russe with blue silk.

The work is finished on the outer edge with a thick cord of blue silk and gold thread.

Figure 49 is intended for a cigar-case; but if widened, it would make a very pretty book or portfolio cover.

The material should be light-brown Russia leather; the wheat-sheaf is embroidered in satin-stitch with dark-brown silk—the stem and light outlines in stalk-stitch with gold thread. The bordering is of gold cord, with a network of dark-brown silk, and stitched with black at all the crossings and centres.

Fig. 50.
MONOGRAM IN GOLD THREAD.

This very pretty monogram is worked with gold thread; the leaves and flowers may be done with silk if preferred.

CHAPTER IX.

APPLIED WORK WITH EMBROIDERY.

APPLIQUÉ, as it is usually called, is the most simple kind of decorative needlework, being nothing more than a pattern cut out of one material and transferred on another. It must, of course, like all fancy-work, be neatly done, with no rough edges or mis-matching figures, and embroidery of some kind is used as a finish; but the same amount of skill and practice is not required as in other artistic work.

When properly done, it is very rich and effective; and it recommends itself by the charming results produced with comparatively little labor. The materials may be of almost any kind; but it is necessary that the ornamental part should harmonize with the foundation. One would not think, for instance, of applying velvet on cotton, or linen—while on satin, it makes the richest kind of applied work.

Appliqué may be fine or coarse according to the purpose for which it is intended; if fine, it is safer to put it in a frame before beginning the work. If the groundwork is velvet, satin, or silk, holland should be stretched in a frame, and the design drawn upon it and upon the velvet or other material; they should then be pasted together, and cut out with a sharp pair of scissors. Cloth and commoner materials do not require this "backing," as it is called; but may be cut after the pattern is traced, and pasted directly on the groundwork.

The gum, or paste, used for this purpose should be as thick and dry as possible, for fear of its coming through and staining the material; and before pasting on cloth or velvet, it will be well to lay the pieces down where they are to be fastened, and view them from various points to see that the pile always goes the same way—or a different shade of color will be the result.

When the material is particularly delicate, isinglass is used instead of paste; and the piece applied should be very carefully smoothed before it is left to dry—as a curved or cross-cut piece is apt to get out of its proper curves or to stretch too much.

With a complicated design, the pattern should be traced on the material, and the duplicate parts numbered that they may fit perfectly together. One way of fastening the edges down is to buttonhole them with a lighter or darker shade of silk than the material applied. The veins of leaves are defined by long stitches, also of a lighter or darker shade.

In the commoner kinds of appliqué, cloth, for instance, on duck, or Turkish towelling, or on cloth of another color, basting will generally answer the purpose of keeping the pattern securely in its place.

Magnificent work is done in appliqué; curtains of gold-colored satin with garnet velvet leaves—the edges defined with a white cord, in which a little blue was mingled; cushions of Moorish arabesques, scarlet velvet on white satin—the velvet edged with gold braid; mantel-lambrequins of brown velvet figures on a groundwork of dead-gold; these suggest endless variations, which a little taste and some eye for color may make beautiful in the extreme.

Ivy leaves are especially satisfactory in this kind of work; and so is any large, clearly-defined figure. The accompanying illustration will be found useful for a bordering. The leaves and flowers are

Fig. 51.—BORDER IN APPLIQUÉ.

made of crimson cloth—the stems and veinings of black embroidery silk. This would be very effective on a gray ground; but any color both of cloth and silk may be used. It would be particularly pretty for a basket or a table-cover.

Our next illustration is

A LAMBREQUIN IN APPLIQUÉ.

Beautiful combinations may be made with white, scarlet, and blue cloth, embroidered with black, gold-colored, and maroon silks, in feather-stitch and point-russe—which are the principal stitches used in this kind of work. For small lambrequins, to decorate baskets and brackets, such combinations are very effective; and the illustration shows a particularly pretty one.

Fig. 52.

The upper part of the lambrequin is of white cloth cut in points, and pinked in a small pointed pattern; the under part, of which the points are larger and pinked in scallops, is of garnet color. On the white points are star-like flowers with buds of blue cloth; and on the claret-colored ones, the same in pink cloth—ornamented with point-

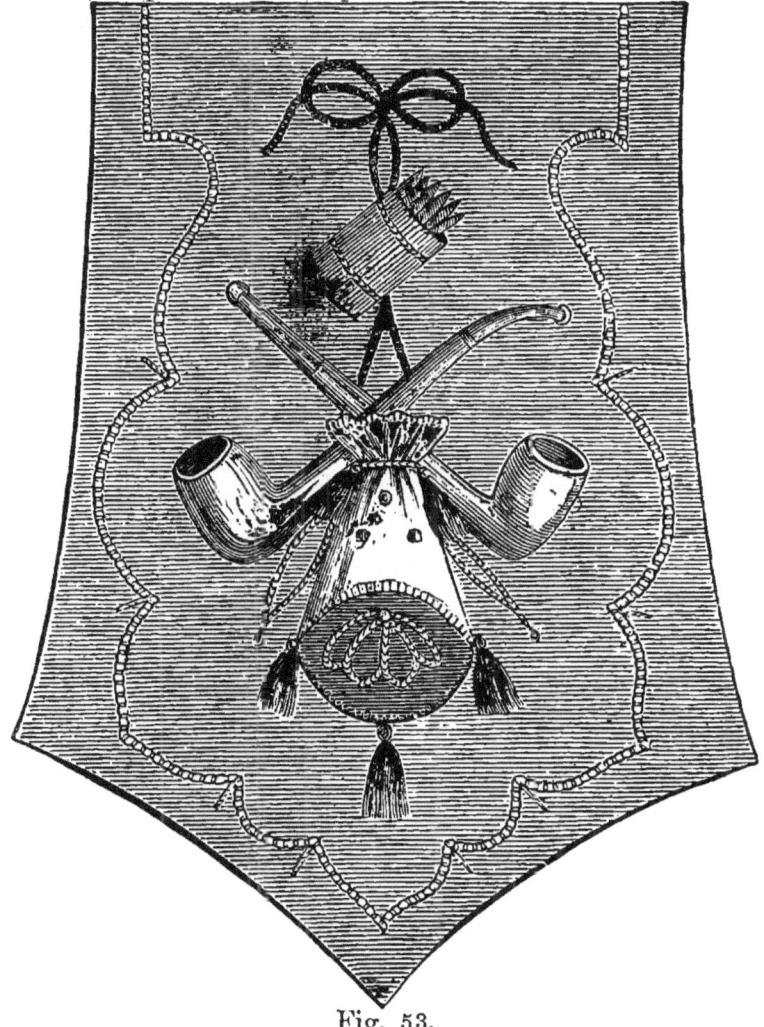

Fig. 53.

russe stitches of silk to match. The middle of each flower is a round piece of yellow cloth fastened with point-russe stitches of red silk.

The stems and sprays are done in stalk, chain, and feather stitches of light green silk.

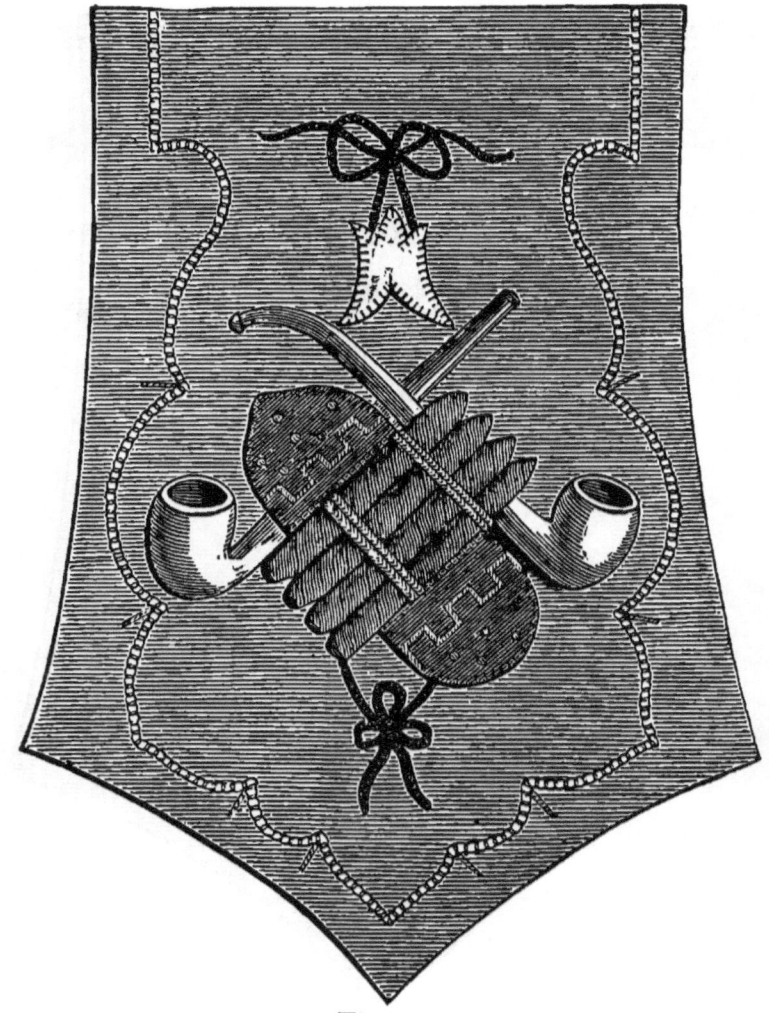

Fig. 54.

The dark points have, near the pinking, a line of twisted buttonhole stitches in maize-colored silk—and the light points have a similar line of red silk. Both are also ornamented with steel beads.

A handsome tobacco pouch may be made from the illustrations, which represent the two patterns used—each side being duplicated.

Four such pieces are cut out of crimson or scarlet cloth, and worked in appliqué. In the first one, the chain-stitch border (not the outer edge) is worked with green silk. The knot from which the different articles are suspended is done with black silk; the cigar-case is of yellow cloth; the cigars worked in satin-stitch with brown silk. The case has two bands of chain-stitch in blue silk, and is edged all round with button-hole stitch in the same color. The pipes are of white cloth shaded with long stitches of gray silk, and edged with yellow. The upper part of the pouch is of blue cloth, with a white silk edging and yellow dots; the under part of brown cloth, with black edging and a pattern worked in chain-stitch with white; the three tassels are embroidered with black and yellow silk.

In the second pattern, the outer border is yellow, the knots black; the small pattern at the top is of blue cloth edged with yellow; the pipes of white cloth edged with blue and shaded with gray. The bundle of cigars is of brown cloth shaded with black stitches, and fastened on with double rows of chain-stitch in yellow silk. The cigar-case is of light green cloth edged with white; the Grecian pattern and dots are embroidered over it with white silk also.

To make the pouch up, join the four pieces together by seams—which are concealed by gold braid; cut out also and join four similar pieces of white kid for the lining; fasten this to the outside at the top only. Sew small brass rings around the top, and run a double piece of crimson silk cord through them. Put silk tassels of various colors at the bottom of the pouch and at each of its four corners.

Appropriate devices for needlebooks, work-baskets, toilet-boxes, etc., may be made from these suggestions; and there is no reason why the small articles in daily use should not be as complete and artistic in their way as more pretentious undertakings. Many who cannot attempt large pieces of work will appreciate these small patterns.

Figure 55 gives a quarter of a very handsome lamp-mat in application and embroidery.

The foundation is a square piece of olive-green cloth, on which is applied a rim of pale-blue cloth two inches wide. The edge is bordered with a thread of dark-blue and light-brown double zephyr worsted, which is overcast on the foundation with fawn-colored silk floss.

Having transferred the outlines of the design to the rim and to the olive-green cloth foundation, as shown in the illustration, work the buds in the centre of the foundation with pale pink and light yellow bourette worsted—and the calyxes with réséda worsted, in two shades, in diagonal button-hole stitch; the loops of which meet in the middle of each leaf, forming the vein. The vines are worked in herring-bone stitch with old gold-colored filling silk. Chain stitches of similar silk define the stems.

On the blue cloth, the flowers are worked with pink and yellow bourette worsted in two shades; and the leaves and calyxes with olive and réséda worsted, in several shades, in diagonal button-hole stitch. The vines and stems are worked in chain-stitch with yellowish-brown filling silk in three shades. The calyxes are defined with satin-stitches

Fig. 55.—Design for Lamp Mats.—Application Embroidery.

of light-yellow filling silk, which are edged with chain-stitches of dark-yellow silk.

The rim is embroidered in point-russe with light-brown double zephyr worsted in the manner shown in the illustration. For the trimming on the outer edge of the mat, overcast a thread of yellow-brown and a thread of light yellow double zephyr worsted in double rows with dark and light yellow silk floss on the foundation in scallops—fill the interval with knotted stitches of pale pink worsted, and border the scallops alternately with a long and a short button-hole stitch of old-gold-colored filling silk. Trim the pinked edge of the foundation with tassels of worsted in the colors of the embroidery.

Fig. 56.—APPLICATION BORDER.

These pretty borders may also be used as strips for afghans and chair-covers.

For Figure 56, a strip of blue cloth an inch and a quarter wide is placed on a foundation of écru linen; and through the middle is run a white braid with horizontal stitches of green, vertical stitches of yellow-brown, and cross-stitches of pink worsted. The blue strip is bordered on both sides with dark-green worsted braid, sewed on with a cross-stitch of light-green worsted, which is wound with maroon worsted. Diagonal stitches of light and dark red worsted, crossed with horizontal stitches of dark-blue worsted, border the braid on the outside.

The border in Figure 57 is made also of écru linen, on which claret-colored braid three-quarters of an inch wide is basted. On the latter, dark-green braid a quarter of an inch wide is fastened with a cross seam of white split filling silk, caught down with black. The crossed stitches on the inner edge of the maroon braid are in blue and gold—the point-russe stitches beyond in scarlet and black.

In the middle of the border, apply round pieces of white cloth with point-russe stitches of green silk; and connect them with vertical stitches of maroon, which are fastened on the foundation at the middle with cross stitches of the same color.

KEY-BAG IN APPLIQUÉ AND EMBROIDERY.

Both sides of this handsome key-bag are given in Figures 58 and 59. It is made of gray kid and lined with gray silk.

On one side is embroidered a key formed of poppies, with their leaves and stems· and at the top of the key is perched an owl. The poppies are worked with five shades of blue-green silk; the plumage of the owl with four shades of brown silk—the shades all blending almost imperceptibly together. The owl's eyes are worked in scarlet and white silk.

The other side of the bag has appliqué figures of steel-colored silk in the form of a Gothic lock. They may be edged either with gold cord or with fine gray silk cord. The screens are done in satin-stitch with silver-gray silk.

After lining each side, the two parts of the bag are joined with a border of gray ribbon, continued around the whole as in the illustrations. It is stitched on with fine gray silk. The bag is fastened with a steel button and a silk loop.

Fig. 57.—Application Border.

Figures 60 and 61 are rich border patterns suitable for table-covers, mats, and brackets. The embroidery is in button-hole, point-russe stitches and knots; the veinings of the leaves in Figure 60 in stalk-stitch and long embroidery stitch. The colors can be arranged to suit the taste of the worker.

SILK APPLIQUÉ WORK.

This is principally used for flowers and leaves; and when care is taken in shading, the effect is almost if not quite equal to embroidery.

The pansy is one of the easiest flowers to imitate in this way—the two upper petals being made of purple silk, and the lower ones of violet, or yellow; with the edges button-holed round, and a few long stitches put in by way of veining.

Rose petals may be beautifully done by selecting silk of the prevailing hue of the petal, and shading with fine embroidery or split

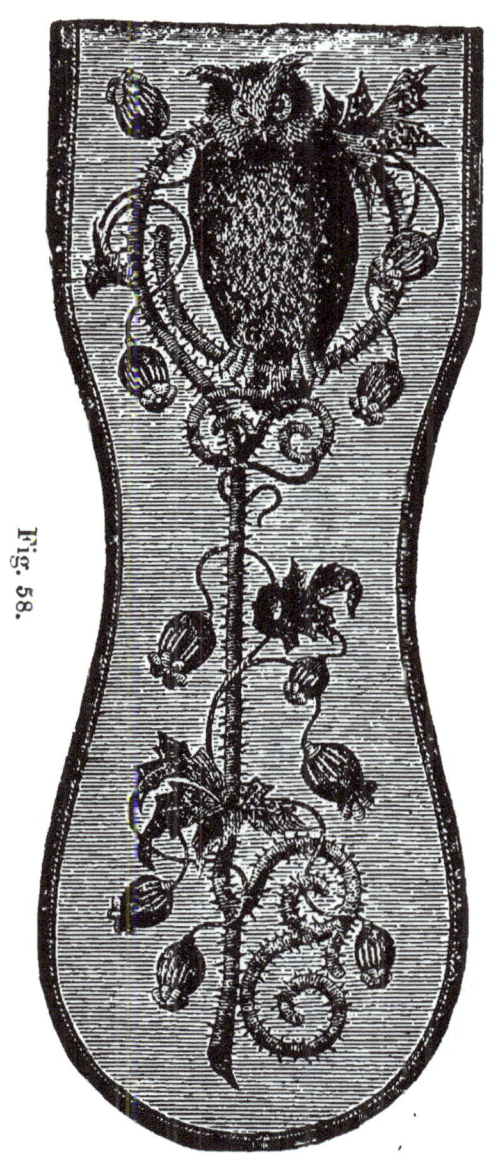

Fig. 58.

filling silk. Stalks and tendrils, and leaf-veinings are worked with embroidery silk.

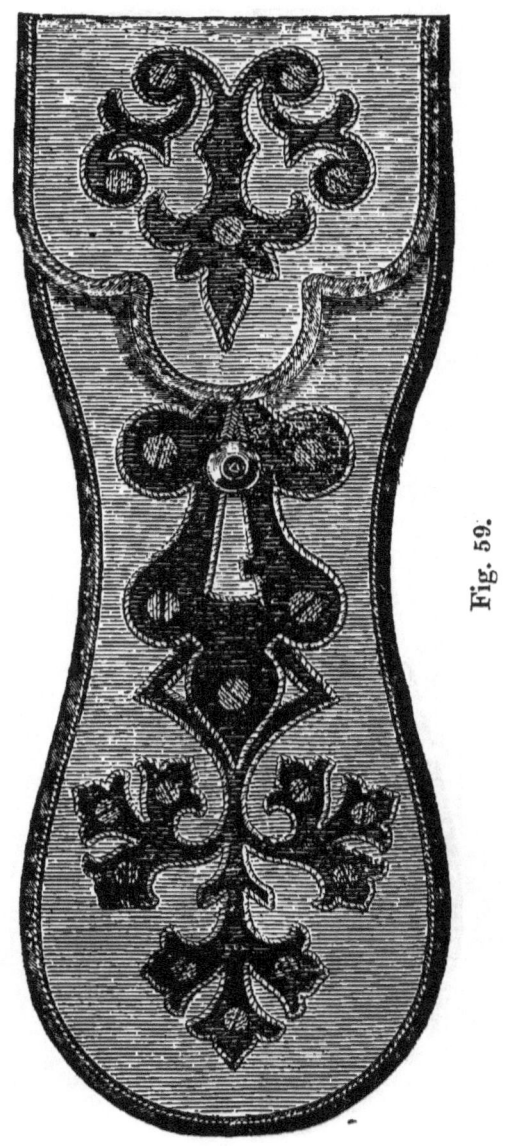

Fig. 59.

A cluster of apple-blossoms is very pretty in this kind of work; and may be done on a ground of pale-blue, gray, or olive. Satin or velvet would make a very handsome foundation. So delicate a piece of work should be done with great care; and besides the edging in button-hole and the long stitches in embroidery-silk, delicate shading is done with filling silk.

The main stems and tendrils are worked in stalk-stitch with green and brown embroidery-silk; where the stems join flower or bud, and for other little finishing touches, satin-stitch is used. The centres of the blossoms are of yellow silk in knot-stitch and common embroidery-stitch.

Silk is sometimes applied on lace with good effect; and the finest specimen known of this work is the beautiful shawl made for the Empress Eugénie, and for some time past on exhibition at Stewart's.

Fig. 60.—Border in Appliqué.

Seen through its glass-case, it is a marvel of coloring and truth to nature; the roses almost perfume the air, and the graceful droop of the wistaria in the centre is perfect. This piece of art-needlework fully deserves its name, and is valued at $100,000; but it is a question if all that weary labor with those minute pieces of silk (so joined on the under side that the points of meeting can be seen only through a magnifying-glass), to say nothing of the cobweb-lace foundation (also hand-made), could possibly be remunerated with money.

CRETONNE-WORK.

The subject of appliqué could not be exhausted without some reference to this popular branch of it—which, when new, was considered the most bewitching fancy-work ever invented.

The most desirable flowers and figures for cretonne-work are to be found in the fine, soft, French cretonne; and the most tiresome part of the work is that which has to be done first—the careful cutting out of these figures with a sharp pair of scissors. They are then to be gummed, or fastened with a few stitches done with fine cotton on the foundation. Much basting is not desirable, as it pulls the material and frays the applied work.

Black satin is a very effective foundation for cretonne-work, as it throws out all the bright and delicate colors; and farmer's-satin answers very nicely. Soft gray and blue silesia are often very satisfactory for this purpose; and a work-basket, made by the writer, of gray silesia, with pink rosebuds and leaves in cretonne-work on each panel, and lined with blue silesia, quite exceeded her expectations.

Workers differ about the best methods of doing cretonne application; some suggesting for the edge a loose buttonhole of rather fine

Fig. 61.—Border in Appliqué.

silk, on the plea that this prevents raggedness and answers the purpose of making the work subservient to the application. But the most approved method is to treat the cretonne merely as a design and a guide to color—covering the flowers and leaves almost entirely with split floss and embroidery silk. A thick outline in satin stitch secures the edges; and the leaves besides being veined are frequently ornamented with small French knots, or short backstitches. Flower-centres are done in French knots.

Chairs and mantels may be handsomely ornamented by a rich stripe of cretonne-work in pink or red roses on a black satin ground; and table-cover borderings may be made in the same way, and attached to the main body. Sofa-cushions, foot-rests, portfolios, and many other things, may be decorated in the same way.

The simpler kinds of appliqué-work have been made very common by the immense number of animals, insects, and figures, such as were never seen in earth, air, or sea, exposed for sale in all the fancy shops, and offering easy inducements to amateurs to fasten them in almost any way upon whatever material their fancy might dictate. The Turkish-towelling fever raged throughout the length and breadth of the land; and although a little of this work, when well done, is very effective, especially in a cottage parlor, it has been carried to such an excess and much of it so bunglingly done, that there is a very general pushing of it aside for something newer.

Dragons and Chinamen, the most popular figures for this kind of work, were never known to infest Turkey; and whatever else we are in fancy-work, it is desirable to be harmonious. Rich arabesques in colored cloth of the true Oriental hues, edged with black to give them greater brilliancy on the pale brown groundwork, would be far more in character; and the inevitable ruche of scarlet braid should be toned down to a more quiet red, or whatever color is most suitable as the key-note.

We may be artistic even with Turkish-towelling and cloth application; but unless we *are* this, let us not be ornamental.

CRAPE PICTURES IN APPLIQUÉ.

Among the newest materials for application-work, are those preposterous representations on a ground of crinkly material known as Chinese pictures. These are of various sizes, and are found now in most of the fancy stores; and although they usually defy all the rules of reason and of color, they are, nevertheless, highly ornamental.

One of these works of art is before us now, divided into four compartments by bands of bright yellow, and tending generally to ornithology on original principles. Two skies are pink, one green, and one yellow; surrounded by the pink sky, a small bird of the sparrow order, with notoriously short legs and unwebbed feet, is walking at ease on some lead-colored water, while a small forest of foliage springs apparently from his back; under the yellow sky, a maize-colored bird on an inky bough opens his mouth evidently at a mulberry a few feet below him. Nemesis is upon him, however, in the shape of a silkworm that is attempting to climb his back. The best that can be said of the mulberries is that they are deeply, darkly, unmistakably purple; and we know them for mulberries because they *are* purple, and because the green leaf cannot be intended for anything else.

The other divisions are perfectly harmonious; and as an art-study, this "bit of color" would not be recommended. Skilfully applied, however, and "touched up" with embroidery, it would be found very ornamental.

Many of these pictures have Chinese or Japanese figures on them; and the confused coloring is best brought out by a frame-work of black velvet ribbon. They make pretty tidies sewn on gray Java canvas, with a bordering of black velvet from two to three inches wide embroidered in feather-stitch—and beyond that an equal width of the canvas worked in a sort of mosaic pattern in point-russe with floss-silks—then a fringe of the canvas, with the different colored silks mixed in, about two inches deep.

Lace is often used as a trimming for these tidies, but it is very unsuitable. Long embroidery stitches of silk, as in cretonne-work, improve these pictures very much; and many of them are so brightly-colored in themselves, that they are as decorative as Chinese fans. They may be used for a variety of purposes; and appliquéd on black velveteen, make handsome hangings for mantels.

LINEN APPLIQUÉ.

Handsome embroidery is sometimes done by working the design on linen, and then applying it to richer materials. The embroidery, when finished, is "backed" by paper before taking it from the frame, to give it firmness; when quite dry, it is taken out and cut carefully round the figures with a sharp pair of scissors, leaving about a sixteenth of an inch as a margin. It must then be laid on the material and tacked down, if the latter is loose—if it is framed, the piece of embroidery should be fastened on it by small pins thrust perpendicularly through it. It must then be more fully secured by sewing it over in small stitches.

The linen edge is covered by a gold or silver cord, fastened down with fine silk matching the cord in color. It is well to paint the back of the embroidery with paste, that the ends of silk may be secured.

A great deal of Eastern embroidery has the look of applied work —being done in the long embroidery-stitch in regular lines from east to west, or *across* the shape to be filled, instead of from north to south; no attempt being made to follow the natural lines of the leaf or flower.

This style has a rich effect in purely conventional forms, but is not suitable for floral designs; a line of black or gold around the figures is nearly always used. We saw some Cretan work lately, that was several hundred years old, done in this way with silk and a sort of flat gold thread on coarse linen; and the effect was very gorgeous.

CHAPTER X.

EMBROIDERY IN CHENILLE.

At one time chenille work was all the fashion. Its beautiful, velvety appearance, and the soft brightness of its colors, made it very effective; but it was an expensive material, and would only bear the most delicate usage.

Silk hand-screens were frequently embroidered with chenille; and in some old-fashioned mansions, such an article of the shape of Figure 62 may be found even now.

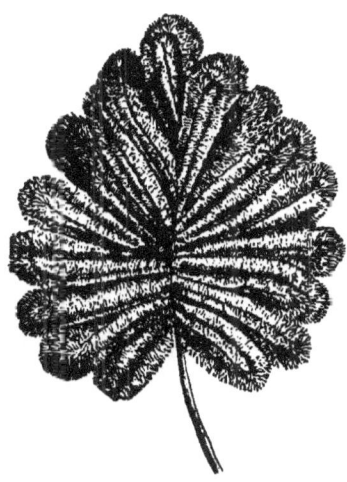

Fig. 62.—Hand-Screen in Chenille.

To do a "piece" in chenille was quite a necessary part of a young lady's education; and these pieces were treated like Miss Linwood's paintings in crewels. They usually represented landscapes; and handsomely framed, and protected by a glass, were hung in a place of honor, as a sort of certificate that the worker was entitled to be pronounced finished.

A performance of this kind that is now cherished as an heirloom, the work of somebody's great-grandmother, consumed a hundred dollars' worth of chenille. It is a mourning-piece: a tomb and two weeping figures in the foreground, the country church, and graveyard. It is very smooth, beautiful work, and has the effect of a painting.

Chenille is still used in a measure for small, ornamental articles; and no material represents moss so well. It is suitable both for flat and raised embroidery; and it may be worked on a variety of materials; but those with smooth surfaces are best suited to its velvet-like appearance.

A needle with a round eye is the proper kind for embroidering with chenille, and this should be large enough not to fray the thread. As it is an expensive material, it should be used economically; and all waste at the back of the work should be avoided by bringing the needle close up to the last stitch and not crossing it on the underside. It is easy to measure or guess the length of the needleful required for working each particular part, and to cut it as short as possible, to prevent the using of the same position again, and also to draw a very small piece through the eye of the needle.

The necessity of making knots may be avoided by working a small stitch or two in the part intended to be covered.

In shaded embroidery, the stitches should not be matted too closely together, as this destroys the velvety appearance of the chenille. It should be more closely shaded than silk embroidery; at least six shades should be used in flowers and leaves.

In flat embroidery, the stitches should be regular, but not closer than to allow the chenille to lie roundly on the surface. It is always pretty edged or mixed with gold.

CHAPTER XI.

SILK EMBROIDERY ON LINEN.

EGYPTIAN embroidery was done on linen or cotton, the threads of the material being almost or entirely pulled out one way, and the remainder embroidered with bright-colored silk. The effect was very rich and showy; but the peculiar art of doing it has been lost.

Some specimens of Egyptian embroidery in the time of the Pharaohs, now in the Louvre, are described as follows: one has narrow red stripes on a broad yellow stripe, wrought with a pattern in needle-work; another piece is on blue, and worked all over in white embroidery, in a kind of netting-pattern, the meshes of which outline irregular cubic shapes.

Silk embroidery on linen is an old fashion revived; and it was used particularly on coverlets and curtains in the form of outline work. This was often done in one color only; and in a bold, set pattern, it was very effective. A more flowing or branching design, well enclosed in lines and borders, looks equally well, with the worker's name or monogram, and the date added.

These coverlets and curtains were sometimes made of Bolton sheeting, rather as a foundation than a ground—being nearly covered with an appliqué pattern of flowers and leaves in cloth, and the stems worked in crewel or silk. The small vacant spaces were often filled with a very simple diaper.

Strong linen makes the best ground for outline work; and a pattern in silk is more durable as well as pleasanter to work. It must be remembered, though, that in silk embroidery for articles that are to be washed, great care must be taken that the embroidery does not fade into one pale, undistinguishable hue.

To prevent this, the silks should first be unwound, cut into pieces of a suitable length, and thrown into boiling water. If, after boiling for several minutes, they retain their color when dried, they may be "warranted not to fade." It is recommended to boil but one shade at a time—using fresh water for each one.

Many useful and pretty things may be made of embroidered linen; and it is particularly pleasant for summer use. Tea-table cloths look well with ends embroidered towel-fashion, or bordered all round—

outline-work being more suitable for this purpose than filled-in embroidery, as it will bear washing better.

Embroidered linen makes very nice tidies; and original designs, or figures from Japanese fans, will often transform these conveniences into works of art. White linen decorated with blue only is very pretty when the other furnishings are blue.

Bedroom hangings are very pleasing in this linen outline-work—also pieces to hang above washstands and borders for brackets.

EMBROIDERED FRUIT DOYLEYS.

These may be made very dainty and charming—suggesting (not filling in) the most perfect little pictures. The skill of the worker should bring out the idea clearly without the aid of detail.

A few descriptions lately met with will furnish illustrations of this kind of work.

A set of very small doyleys, about six inches square, had the edges ravelled out in fringe nearly an inch deep—the border serged with fine thread to keep the flowing strands in place. Half an inch from this, and half an inch in width, were a number of threads drawn out all around, giving the appearance of an insertion. The cross threads were then drawn backwards and forwards over each other, four strands at a time, and stayed with one row of thread, like the old-fashioned herring-bone—forming a cross at each corner.

In the centre of each doyley was embroidered with Japanese silk a cup and saucer, a teapot, a pitcher, etc., in graceful forms, and soft, shaded colors—all according to the design and taste of the embroiderer. They were scarcely more than outlines—the impression given being more of quiet artistic beauty than of the object represented.

On another little doyley is sketched a slender Indian jar; beside it, a bed of reeds, or water-grasses, seems to sway and rustle in summer airs—so pliant are the stems, so free the groupings. As if just risen from this cool quietude, a flight of birds soars upwards and away.

The jar is wrought in gold-color, red, blue, and soft drab. A few bars, ovals, dots, and lines indicate the rich decoration. The reeds which, of course, are not shaded, are done in brown and a dull green. The rising birds are dark blue. It hardly need be said that both reeds and birds are conventionalized—the reeds being the slenderest shadows, and the birds mere converging lines.

Directions for this kind of work are given as follows:

Select close, even linen, of the kind used for sheeting, and a yard and a half in width, and be careful to see that it has no uneven threads; half a yard and one inch, the latter to allow for shrinkage and uneven ends, is sufficient for one dozen doyleys. Have it washed in strong, boiling-hot suds, well rinsed, and then boiled in clear water to remove the starch and render it pliable; rinse from clear cold water, and put it to dry without any addition of bluing.

When dry, cut off the selvedge; and pull a thread at top and bottom that it may be cut perfectly straight. Do not attempt to cut any part of the work without first pulling a thread as a guide, for it is impossible to have it perfectly regular either by creasing it or by following an unpulled thread.

Divide the linen into two pieces, each of which will be a quarter of a yard in width, by a yard and a half in length. Each of these pieces is to be cut into six—giving twelve pieces, each nine inches square. Ravel them all around until you have a fringe seven-eighths of an inch in depth; it is better to make a faint pencil-mark on each of the four sides before commencing, that the fringe may be perfectly even. With No. 100 unwaxed cotton and a fine needle, whip them around— taking up four or five threads on the needle at once, and having the stitches as even and regular as possible; do not use knots, but run the cotton along at beginning and end—commencing with a thread long enough for the whole side, and avoid catching the fringe in the work.

Place the doyley straight before you, and with a rather coarse needle mark a point seven-eighths of an inch from both the upper and left-hand sides—then mark a point half an inch below this one, and parallel with the left-hand side of the doyley; with a pair of sharp-pointed scissors cut the linen from point to point.

Turn the linen around so that the left-hand side shall be the upper one, and the lower at the left hand; cut a slit in this corner corresponding to the other, and continue until each corner has been cut. It would be better to practice the cutting on a piece of paper first; and when you find the cutting at each corner is at right angles with the one below it, the work is right. With the needle-point pull a thread loose at the top and bottom of the slit cut, drawing it along until you come within three-eighths of an inch of the slit cut in the other corner. Cut the linen from thread to thread, and repeat at the other three corners. When finished, there will be eight cuts in the doyley —the two on each side parallel to each other.

With No. 80 unwaxed cotton, button-hole around each one as neatly as possible; then pull out all the threads on each side that were made free by the cutting. These threads are now to be herring-boned, using a fine needle and the same cotton; this is done by commencing at one end of the threads, and taking up four threads on the needle, draw the cotton through them, bringing it up at right angles to the work; take another stitch in the same place, only catching the body of the linen slightly with the needle and cotton.

Repeat this until you come to the other end—when, turning the doyley upside down, commence taking up the threads again on the needle, only taking two threads from each cluster of the row before;

this makes a sort of ladder-work in the border, much prettier than if the threads were taken in corresponding clusters.

When they have all been herring-boned, the fascinating work of decoration begins. For silk, letter D button-hole twist is the most satisfactory in all colors, except shades of red and green. There are four shades of blue: navy that is almost black, a navy that is bright, a bright sky blue, and a very delicate one; brown of two shades; gold-color, lemon, and two shades of sage-green. Bright red shading on scarlet, and entirely free from a Solferino tint, deep and bright rose peach blossom, and a turquoise-blue are best when on quills.

Having boiled and dried the silk, it will be found in using it that it is three-stranded; but it must be separated and only one strand used in working. This should be carefully moistened when it becomes flossy and uneven. Green is the most difficult color to manage; and it is only the old-fashioned apple-green found in skeins that will be at all satisfactory.

The designs should be drawn on the doyleys with a sharp lead-pencil—being careful not to soil the work by wrong outlines and erasing. If the latter is necessary, it is better to wash out the marks with warm water and soap than to use any other method; and then begin outlining again.

A set done in fans, of different shapes and decoration, are as pretty as one could desire. If it is impossible to draw from one lying before you; cut a pattern in pasteboard and outline with the pencil. The different periodicals occasionally give beautiful styles of fans; and the cheap Japanese fans are very suggestive in the way of color and figure.

Outline them in bright blue, with an inner line of pink; navy with light blue; sage green with pink; or any other colors that contrast or harmonize; make the stick and ribs of bamboo color, or gold. An open fan is beautiful outlined in gold, sticks and all; with sprays of star-shaped flowers done in red, stems in gray, and leaves in green. These flowers, etc., are only outlined, not done in the solid satin-stitch, and should be as delicate as possible.

The stitch called Kensington is used; and is the one familiar to all embroiderers, in both flannel and muslin, as stem-stitch. The needle is kept with the point toward the worker; and you are constantly working from you.

Very quaint and pretty designs can be taken from Japanese print-plates, tea-trays, and cabinets. Two fans, one-fourth open, the one in the middle, the other at one corner, are very effective; but when an open fan is used, one is sufficient for a doyley.

A spider's web, hanging from a branch just coming over one side of the doyley, is extremely pretty. Outline the stems in gray, leaves in green, and the web in light-blue—making it out perfectly round, but longer one way than another; have some of the rays to project a little, others caught on the branches—and from one of the lower ones a spider dangling, while in the rib a stitch or two of black makes a good representation of his prey. Give a little color in one of the lower corners by a few rushes—one or two of which should have a few red tassels.

An apple-bough with a leaf of green here and there; tiny flowers of red and pink, some of which have drifted off before a gentle wind, make beautiful designs; but when one's eyes are open to them, it is astonishing how many ideas are gathered here and there that would otherwise be lost. A walk among one's flowers, a border in a magazine or art-journal, will give suggestions in some form or other.

The cold marble of one's dressing-table or bureau loses its cheerless aspect by the color one of these covers gives it. A piece of linen a yard and a half long and three-eighths in width, should be fringed an inch and a half at front and back, with a much deeper one at the ends. Work a border an inch deep, a quarter of a yard from the herring-bone at each end, and meeting the herring-bone at the sides.

Use red, bright gold, and light blue, with a touch here and there of navy blue. A spray of wistaria at one end, and apple-blossoms at the other, are very pretty. Tray-covers should be from a yard square to seven-eighths one way, and a yard the other. Fringe and herring-bone them, decorating only the corners, as the centre is so covered that decoration would be lost.

These very explicit directions have been taken almost entire from a late periodical; and will be found so full and satisfactory, that almost any needlewoman, on reading them, might successfully attempt this pretty work.

CHAPTER XII.

HOLBEIN WORK.

This is a simple and truly artistic kind of needle-work, chaste and elegant in design and correct in style; its beauty depending not upon strong contrasts or striking patterns, but on its exquisite finish and neatness.

Holbein work is a kind of linen decoration with colored threads; and was highly popular several centuries ago. Lingerie table-linen, towels, and bed-linen, were thus adorned in a charming and tasteful manner; and as instruction in this branch of needlework, of which so few remnants remain, is chiefly given through the master works of the younger Holbein, it has been named from him.

This great painter has reproduced the embroidery with wonderful fidelity, showing plainly its charming peculiarity of being alike on both sides. It differs in this respect from all other embroidery, except that of some Oriental nations, and has literally no wrong side to show, and requires, therefore, no lining to conceal defects. "Divers colors of needlework *on both sides*," is the oldest kind of ornamental needlework of which there is any mention.

To accomplish this work on both sides is by no means difficult, as might at first be supposed; and many articles for which no other kind of embroidery would be appropriate may be very tastefully ornamented with Holbein work. The effect is that of colored lines on a white ground after the fashion of a pen-drawing—the design being equally distinct on both sides.

The foundation for this embroidery is usually white linen Java canvas, which washes better, and is of smoother and firmer texture than cotton canvas. If linen canvas cannot be obtained, the ordinary cotton canvas, or colored Java canvas, may be used instead.

A piece of canvas, a canvas needle with a dull point, red Turkish cotton No. 30, or else several threads of colored or black silk (somewhat coarser than ordinary sewing-silk), are all that is required for Holbein work.

No knot should be made, to look ugly on the under side, in the beginning; and to avoid this, insert the needle between the double layer of the threads of the canvas, so that the working thread is con-

ARTISTIC EMBROIDERY. 87

cealed on both sides; let the end of the thread project a little, so that it may be held in the hand, pass the needle around one of the four threads forming a square (with the ordinary cotton canvas, only *half* of a thread should be caught), carry it back the same way it was inserted (see Figure 63), and draw the stitch tight—at the same time holding fast the projecting thread.

Fig. 63.

The single thread on which the working thread is fastened is drawn in between the double threads of the canvas in tightening the stitch, so that the latter is not visible on either side. The manner of doing this is shown in Figure 34.

Then work the second stitch (see Figure 64) similarly to the first; but underneath the nearest threads running in an opposite direction, draw the stitch tight, so that it is concealed; and then repeat the first stitch once more completely, in order to fasten the thread securely. After working these three stitches, the thread should be quite firm; and the fastening should scarcely be visible.

Cut off the projecting end of thread close to the canvas, and begin the embroidery. To work a straight line, as in Figure 65, make a horizontal stitch of two squares of the canvas, pass over two squares, work another horizontal stitch on the following two squares—and continue the first row in this way, always taking up two squares for one stitch, as shown by Figure 66. This is called running stitch.

When the line has been worked of the length desired, for instance, ten stitches, there will be five running stitches and five intervals on

Fig. 64.

each side; and the stitches on one side will always come on the intervals of the other side. In order to close the line, and fill all intervals,

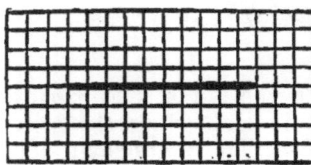

Fig. 65.

work, going back, just as in the first row (see Figure 67), which completes the line, and brings the working thread back to the point where the work was begun. This point is always indicated by * in the illustrations.

Work this straight line, consisting of *ten* stitches, from right to left in the order of the figures given in Figure 67. Only the upper stitches are counted and numbered; but, as a matter of course, the other side of the work is to present the same appearance as the side on which it is done. The

Fig. 66.

regularity of the work will be increased if, in working straight lines, the needle is always, in the second row, inserted underneath, and drawn out above the threads in the first row; in this way the threads

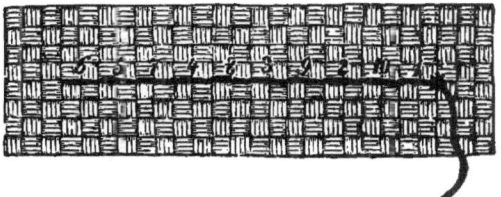

Fig. 67.

of both rows are regularly intertwined, and the stitches are slightly slanting, as plainly shown in the last illustration.

A diagonal line, as in Figure 68, is worked similarly to the straight line, except that instead of crossing two squares in a straight direction, they are taken up diagonally, as in ordinary cross-stitch. The first stitch, therefore, exactly resembles half of a cross-stitch; and between the first and second stitches, an interval of the same number of threads remains, which forms half of a cross-stitch on the other side. The line a, Figure 69, shows the first row of a diagonal line of five stitches; and the line b shows this line finished by the second row.

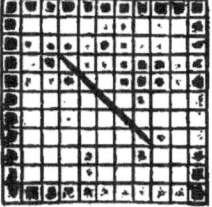

Fig. 68.

For the zigzag line in Figure 70, take a diagonal stitch upward over two squares of the canvas, pass over two squares, and insert the needle downward diagonally in the opposite direction;

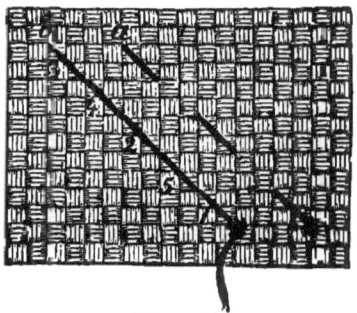

Fig. 69.

take another diagonal stitch upward; and continue in this manner, as shown by a in Figure 71. In the first row, all the stitches on both sides appear slanting to the left. In working the second row, going back, fill all the intervals, as indicated by the figures on the line *b* in Figure 71.

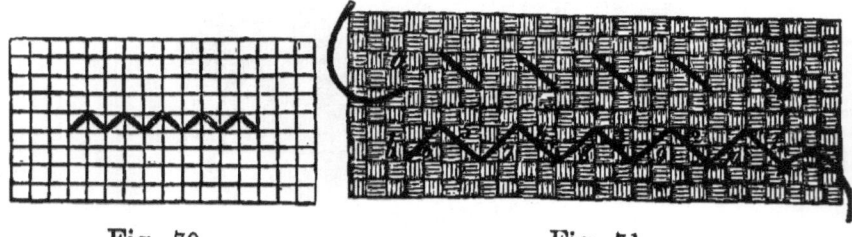

Fig. 70. Fig. 71.

For the Greek line in Figure 72, take a vertical stitch downward over two squares, pass over two squares in a horizontal direction, take a second vertical stitch upward over two squares, so that the stitches

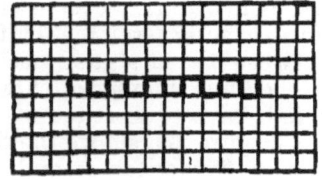

Fig. 72.

always inclose four squares. In this design, all vertical stitches come on the upper side (and all horizontal stitches, consequently, on the under side) in the first row, as shown by *a* in Figure 73; while in filling the intervals in the second row the order is reversed, and all

Fig. 73.

horizontal lines come on the upper side, and the vertical lines on the under side. The line *b*, in Figure 73, shows the Greek line in course of work, and indicates by figures the order in which the stitches should be taken.

For the stair line in Figure 74, work a horizontal stitch from right to left on two squares, pass the needle straight down under two squares, and draw it out; repeat this three times, and then work three stitches upward again. In this design all the horizontal stitches come on the upper side, and all vertical stitches on the under side in the first row, which is shown by *a* in Figure 75; while *b* shows the lines finished by the second row, and indicates the order of stitches by figures.

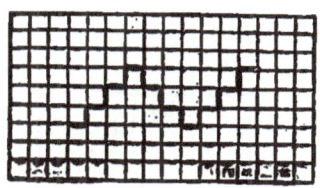

Fig. 74.

The thread, which is always carried back to the point where the work is begun, should be sewn in firmly, as described for the beginning, so that the fastening cannot be detected, and then cut off close to the canvas.

Fig. 75.

These simple designs being mastered, the learner is now prepared for more ambitious efforts; and the lines are frequently divided into branches richly ornamented, that form complicated patterns, and require some study to make both sides of the work alike.

The patterns now consist no longer of simple lines, but of long lines with short ones branching off from them, which may be called main lines and branches.

The design in Figure 76 consists of a main line with upright branches, which is worked in rounds going back and forth, and is thus completed in two rows; no stitch should be omitted on either side, nor should any stitch appear double; and the working thread should always return to the point where the work was begun.

Figure 77 shows the manner of working the first row of this design, the needle indicating how to take the last upright stitch.

Begin the line from *, so that an interval always remains between every two stitches, and work to the point where the line branches off. These branches are worked separately, and are completed in two rows; so that in working the second row of the main line no attention need be paid to them.

Fig. 76.   Fig. 77.

Figure 78 shows the same design finished by the second round; the order of stitches is indicated by figures.

The same rules apply to design 79—which shows a main line with stair-line branches meeting the main line always at two points. In this case, too, the branches are always finished separately before working the main line beyond the point from which the stair-branches proceed.

Fig. 78.   Fig. 79.

Figure 80 shows the first row of this design; the first branch being finished, and the second in course of execution.

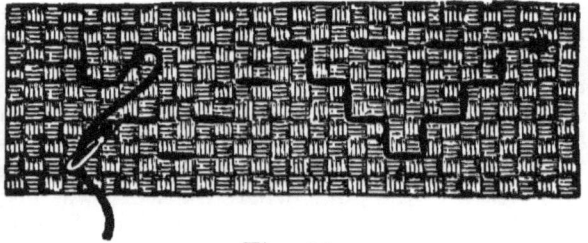

Fig. 80.

Figure 81 shows the design finished by the second round, the figures indicating how to take the stitches. The fact that the branches intersect the main line at two points does not affect the work in the least.

Fig. 81.

Sometimes the branches of the main lines are again furnished with smaller branches, as shown by the forked design in Figure 82.

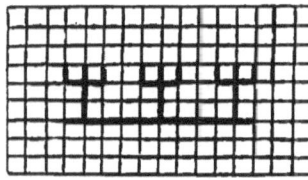

Fig. 82.

In this case, the smaller branches are also worked separately from the point from which they proceed; but the middle line is worked similarly to a main line; working first one row with intervals, next forming the smaller branches or prongs, and then, going back, filling the intervals of the middle line, and returning to the main line.

Figure 83 shows the first row of this design and one of the branches just begun; Figure 84 shows the design finished, and the order of stitches indicated by figures. From time to time, it will be well to glance on the under side and see that the design appears precisely the same as on the right side, which will

Fig. 83.

always be the case when the stitches are worked exactly in the order given in the illustrations.

Frequently the smaller lines branch off from the main line in opposite directions, as shown by Figure 85. In this design the forked

Fig. 84.

figure appears on one side, and the stair-line on the other side—both meeting at one point of the main line.

With such patterns, begin with the main line and work to the point

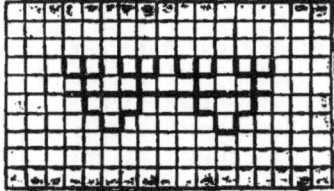

Fig. 85.

where the branches begin—always working these separately. It is immaterial which of the two branches is worked first; but they should both be finished in the first row, so that, in the second row, only the intervals in the main line need be filled. As a general rule, it is well to complete as much of the pattern as possible in the first row.

As Figure 85 is formed by a combination of figures similar to those shown in Figures 65 and 66, it will only be necessary to refer to the description of those figures to enable the worker to execute this design with ease.

Fig. 86.

Fig. 87.

Tree figures, shown in illustration 86, are worked so that the trunk forms the main line, and all the small lines the branches; but the main line should be worked to the point without the branches, the latter being formed in the second row going back. Thus the trunk, forming the middle line, will serve as a guide for placing the branches. Figure 87 shows the manner of working such a figure, the stitches being indicated as usual by numbers.

Each individual design requires separate sewing in of the thread; all connected lines, on the contrary, are worked without interruption.

The working thread should always be taken as long as possible; and when it is used up, it should either be carefully sewed in, as described in the beginning, or it should be fastened to the new thread by means of a weaver's knot. This knot has the advantage of being made small and strong at the same time.

Fig. 88.

Sufficient instructions have now been given to enable the beginner to do a very creditable piece of Holbein work; and Figure 88 is a particularly easy pattern for a towel-border that may be done in red or blue cotton or silk.

Fig. 89.   Fig. 90.

The towel may be made of heavy linen sheeting; or a bordering of linen embroidered in this way may be applied to either end of a damask towel with a line of feather-stitch. Sufficient material should be allowed for a deep, tied fringe.

This pattern will also be found pretty for a bureau or dressing-table cover, as well as a variety of other articles.

Figures 89 and 90 are very effective both for towels and covers.
Holbein work is frequently mixed with cross-stitch and satin-stitch, which give it a richer effect; and for elaborate designs, this is a great improvement. Figures 91, 92, and 93, show very handsome towels embroidered in this way.

These towels are made of a piece of linen sixty-eight inches long and seventeen inches wide, embroidered in cross-stitch and Holbein work with blue or red cotton. The towels are trimmed besides with an open-work design and knotted fringe, and are hemmed narrow on the sides with a cross seam of the colored cotton.

To make a towel, work eight inches from the bottom a rich design in Holbein embroidery, and edge it on both sides with a narrow border in cross-stitch embroidery. Each cross-stitch is worked over two threads in height, and the same in width. Above this border, at

Fig. 93.

a distance of an inch, ornament the towel in a design worked in cross-stitch over canvas with colored cotton.

After finishing the embroidery, draw out the threads of the canvas, and between the borders execute an open-work design. For this, draw out always four threads of the linen lengthwise and crosswise, letting the same number of threads stand, and overcast them diagonally, first in one direction, and then, crossing the same square in the opposite direction; and finish the edge of the borders adjoining the open-work design with button-hole stitches.

Underneath the narrow border, draw out the crosswise threads of the linen, and knot the lengthwise threads to form fringe, as shown in the illustrations.

Fig. 94.—Embroidered Burlaps Portière.

Handsome portières and curtains may be made of burlaps ornamented with Holbein and other embroidery.

For the design in Figure 94, draw out eight threads, each two inches and a half and five inches and three-quarters from the outer edge; cross every eight of the threads left standing, and run them with gold soutache. Between these open-work patterns work the border (see Figure 94) in satin-stitch with light and dark red filling silk; and in Holbein work with light and dark olive-green filling silk.

The open-work pattern is edged with point-russe stitches of dark brown and fawn-colored silk, and cross-stitches of dark red silk.

CHAPTER XIII.

CHURCH EMBROIDERY.—PART I.

The general rules for artistic needlework apply equally well to church embroidery, which is, nevertheless, a distinctive art. In ancient times its magnificence was unparalleled—the worker feeling privileged in working for God's service, and anxious to spare neither time nor expense on their labor.

This branch of decorative needlework has "narrow limitations, stricter laws of fitness, bonds of symbolism, rules of color, and traditions of style; but a student of art needlework will no find these stricter laws prevent church work from being beautiful and harmonious; indeed, they will be aids rather than hindrances; while the knowledge already acquired of general principles of color and design will be a safeguard against placing vulgar, crude, or tasteless combinations where, in many eyes, they would be not only ugly, but irreverent.

It has been well said that, in this kind of work, unity of design and harmony of color take a new and deeper meaning; and honesty of workmanship becomes a duty; while a new reason for conventionalism is seen when we remember that we ourselves, when in God's house, lay aside an ordinary and natural demand.

The descriptions of the richly-embroidered ecclesiastical vestments: robes, sandals, girdles, tunics, vests, palls, altar-cloths, and veils or hangings of various kinds, that were common in churches in the Middle Ages, would almost surpass belief if the minuteness with which they are enumerated in some ancient authors did not attest the fact.

The cost of many of these articles was enormous, for pearls and precious stones were literally interwoven with the needlework, and an almost incredible amount of time and labor was bestowed on them. Several years would frequently be spent on one garment; and some magnificent ninth century vestments are described, which Pope Paschal presented to different churches.

One of these was an altar-cloth of Tyrian purple, having in the middle a picture of golden emblems, with the faces of several martyrs surrounding the Saviour. The cross was wrought in gold, and had round it a border of olive-leaves most beautifully worked. Another had golden emblems, and was ornamented with pearls.

This same pope had a robe worked with gold and gems, with the history of the Ten Virgins with lighted torches beautifully related. He had another of Byzantine scarlet with a worked border of olive-leaves. He had also a robe of woven gold, worn over a cassock of scarlet silk; and another of amber hue embroidered with peacocks in all the brilliant and mysterious shades of their plumage.

Modern church needlework is much more simple and less expensive, and with an ordinary amount of skill and patience and attention to rules and details, almost any embroiderer can accomplish very satisfactory results.

Coarse, prepared linen or muslin, made very stiff, is first stretched in a frame, and the material to be embroidered carefully tacked or pinned on it. This makes a firm ground for working, and gives body to the article to be embroidered. The silk or calico lining is to be placed on the other side of the muslin.

A well-made frame is another important point; and four-piece frames, or frames without stands, formed of two bars with webbing to which the material is sewn, and two laths or stretchers, with holes to receive the pegs, will be found most suitable for this kind of work. They are fastened with screws, and the sizes generally needed range from 20 inches to 6 feet 4 inches.

Figure 95 represents one of these four-piece frames, in which a piece of linen is stretched, and upon it the central figure of an altar frontal in progress of work. It is better not to stretch the frame more than 20 inches at a time, as it is very fatiguing, for a continuance, to take a longer reach than 10 inches from each side bar of the ame.

Great care must be taken not to rub over the material while working; and for this purpose a cambric handkerchief, or an equivalent of soft paper, should be laid upon it. The needlework should always be covered with a soft clean cloth whenever it is left, no matter for how short a space of time.

IMPLEMENTS NEEDED.

The implements used for church embroidery are needles, pins, stiletto, scissors, thimbles, and the *piercer* for manipulating gold. This latter article is as necessary as the scissors in regulating bullion and other materials, as it is rounded and pointed at one end like a small stiletto, and wider and flat-sided at the other.

Round-eyed sharps, from 7 to 2, are the needles most likely to be required for every kind of silk ; the first principally for sewing-silk, the others for crochet and other coarse silks. The best rule for size is to be able to thread a needle instantly, and to draw the needle backwards and forwards through the eye, without the least friction.

Fig. 95.—Four-Piece Frame.

An experienced worker will choose a needle very large in proportion to the thread it is to hold in preference to a smaller one.

The stiletto is used in many ways, a steel one being the best. The ends of stiff cords should be put through holes made by this instrument; and occasions for its use are constantly arising.

Short pins are needed for transferring designs, instead of basting; and in appliqué work, every part of it is carefully arranged by pinning before the process of sewing begins. Cardboard patterns, too, for modern embroidery, are kept in place by this means.

Two thimbles are needed, as the use of both hands is particularly necessary in this kind of work. Thimbles worn a little smooth are preferable, as the roughness of a new thimble catches the silk.

Sharp, strong *nail scissors* will be found most serviceable, and they should be as large in the bows as possible to secure the thumb and finger from hurt in cutting out cardboard designs and textile materials for appliqué.

STITCHES.

The stitches used in ancient ecclesiastical embroidery are found on examination to be quite simple, yet capable of producing the most beautiful effects.

In using gold thread, for instance, it was seldom pulled *through* the foundation, but couched: laid on the surface and sewed down, two or three threads at a time, by stitches taken either somewhat irregularly, or with such method as to produce by a series of them a perfect diapered pattern of color on a gold ground. Figure 96 is an example of what is known as plain couching.

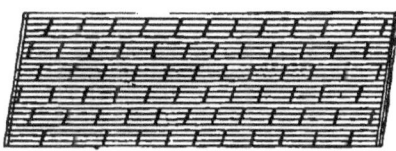

Fig. 96.—PLAIN COUCHING.

Gold-colored embroidery silk has an almost equally rich effect by making three or four parallel lines with it, and working the cross stitches in the contrasting color.

Wavy couching is as easy as plain, the undulated first line regulating the position of the others to any extent.

Diaper couching is another variety often used in old church embroidery for representing pavements, and frequently for backgrounds to emblems, and figures of saints.

Diamond couching is very pretty, and useful for holding down silk, as well as passing, in the ornamentation of large fleur-de-lis, or other conventional forms. The illustration (see Figure 100) is a

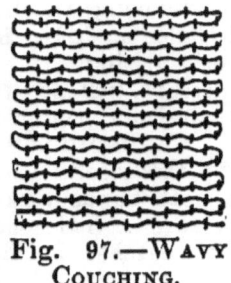
Fig. 97.—Wavy Couching.

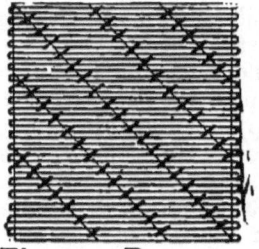
Fig. 98.—Diagonal Couching.

diamond of four stitches each way. The size of the diamond depends upon the dimensions of the space to be covered.

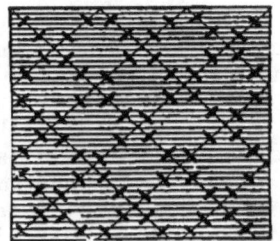
Fig. 99.—Diaper Couching.

The line and cross diaper will be found desirable for covering large spaces with a diapering of needlework. It also makes a very pretty

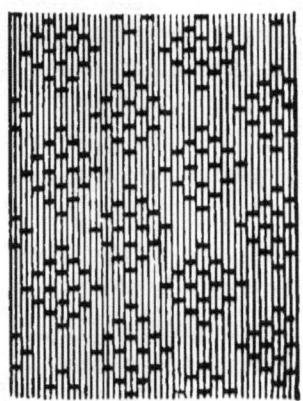
Fig. 100.—Diamond Couching.

border to enclose a plain ground in which a cross or other design is worked. This pattern is most effective when done with lines of passing caught down at their intersections by a cross of crimson or other bright-colored silk. The dots in the centre may be made either with gold beads or French knots.

Fig. 101.—LINE AND CROSS DIAPER.

Various other combinations will suggest themselves in couching; which is one of the most charming and useful methods in the whole range of embroidery.

BASKET-STITCH.

This is another very effective device, and is particularly ingenious. It is used principally for straight borders, or for the raised parts of a conventional crown, a large monogram, or for any pattern of a formal outline where a plaited and interlaced effect is the aim.

To work a border in basket-stitch, any even number of rows of twine, from four upwards, must first be sewn firmly down upon the framed foundation; and over this the gold is to be carried two threads at a time. The worker begins by taking two threads of passing and stitching them down, first over *one* row of twine, then over *two* rows, and over two again, till the single row at the opposite side is reached.

Any number of threads may be carried across in this way before altering the arrangement of sewing down, according to the width decided upon for the divisions of the plait. Say that six threads, or three layers of passing, have been turned backwards and forwards, and caught down precisely alike; the gold is then to be sewn over *two* lines of twine, *each* time, from side to side of the border, for *three* layers more; and so *alternated* to any extent.

Medium purse silk is best for sewing down the gold; and a close, firm twine, like whipcord, should be used for the lines. The thickness of the twine must be governed by the size of the figure or space that the basket-work is intended to cover.

The border should be finished on each side by a gold or silk cord, or an edging of some kind to hide the looped ends of the passing, which are not pulled through, but turned backwards and forwards as evenly as possible.

FLOSS-SILK.

For large leaves, spaces in scrolls, draperies of figures, or foregrounds, long loose lines of colored floss, secured at intervals by single threads of passing laid across, produce a very good effect. Below is the simple *long-stitch*, upon which principle all floss-silk embroidery is wrought. It is the petal of a flower worked in two distinct shades of

Fig. 102.—LONG-STITCH.

blue, and edged with amber crochet-silk sewed down with white. The light shade is to be used first—beginning from the outer edge of the centre of the petal, and working first to one side and then to the other. Then the dark shade is to be worked in like manner *downwards*.

Fig. 103.—SCROLL WITH PASSING.

Figure 103 shows a scroll in *twist-stitch* enriched by passing. The twisted effect is produced by working stitches of an even length one behind the other on an even line. The passing is couched after the silk scroll is worked.

CHAPTER XIV.

CHURCH EMBROIDERY.—PART II.

ALTAR-COVERS have often been made in a style of great magnificence, and are the most costly articles of church embroidery. It is not necessary in a small work like this to give one entire, especially as many modern Gothic churches have richly-carved stone or wooden altars for which only a super-frontal of needlework is required.

Fig. 104.—SUPER-FRONTAL IN FLEUR-DE-LIS.

The fleur-de-lis pattern in Figure 104 is both simple and effective; and wrought in white and gold would be in good taste on either a green or crimson ground.

The embroidery is done in couching—the fleur-de-lis and the curved stems in gold twist-silk, sewed down with orange. The bands of the fleur-de-lis and the trefoils between in white twist-silk, sewed down with gold color. The white to be edged with white cord, the gold color with gold cord.

The fringe is gold color mixed with the color of the ground.

A conventionalized rose is given in Figure 105, full size, to be used in the bordering of a super-frontal.

It is edged with gold cord and worked in two shades of pale pink floss, long embroidery-stitch. The central ring is of bright green silk

Fig. 105.—Rose for Super-Frontal.

the diamonds it encloses gold-color couched on a pale green ground;

the rays, deep rose-color, in long stitches. The outer lines are long, loose stitches in gold thread.

The leaves are in two shades of olive green floss in long embroidery-stitch; the stem, scroll, and finish are in two shades of olive brown, edged with gold thread. This part may be done in couching.

The roses may be in divisions separated by gold-colored lace, or alternated with annunciation lilies.

Fig. 106.—READING-DESK WITH HANGING.

PULPIT, OR DESK HANGINGS.

These are often needed where no altar covering is used; and are much simpler in construction. Figure 106 shows a reading-desk draped; Figure 107 gives a suitable design for the centre; and Figure 108 a very pretty bordering.

The cross and lettering of the central figure are to be done in gold thread, or gold-colored silk, and edged with black. On a white or crimson ground this would be very effective; and it has the advantage of harmonizing with any ground color. It may also be done in appliqué, instead of embroidery.

The border pattern may also be done in gold, or in a mixture of gold and white.

Fig. 107.—Monogram for Desk Hanging.

Fig. 108.—Border for Desk Hanging.

Figure 109 gives a rich pattern in full size for the border of an ante-pendium, or desk-hanging. It is embroidered on white silk rep with silver and gold thread; and sewn on over a black velvet, rep, or

Fig. 109.—Border in Appliqué and Embroidery.

cloth centre. The dark patterns are worked in appliqué with black velvet; the two other shades in gold and silver brocade.

The embroidery is done in satin-stitch with gold and silver braid, silk and cord of the same material.

The border can be worked upon the material for the centre if it is not intended to contrast with it. The pattern can also be worked entirely in silk with satin-stitch.

CHURCH BOOK MARKERS.

These are comparatively easy of execution, although to be done according to the same rules which govern other church needlework. They are made of plain rich ribbon, varying in width from one to three inches, in the five ecclesiastical colors of crimson, blue, green, white, and violet.

Nothing elaborate in the way of embroidery should be attempted on such small articles. A Latin cross on one end, and a simple monogram on the other, are always suitable. Or words such as "Creed" and "Collect," as suited to particular parts of the service, may be worked at the separate ends, in plain Old English letters, surmounted by a Greek cross.

The length of the marker depends upon the size of the book for which it is required. A yard, not including fringe, is the ordinary length. This makes a double marker, as it can be divided in the middle by a barrel or register, to fall over two pages of the book.

A very good contrivance for this purpose is a piece of ivory, of the width of the back of the book, pierced with holes, through which pieces of silk braid, from which the ribbon is suspended, may be inserted and tied. The pieces of ribbon may measure less than half a yard, as the suspender, which should be of stout silk braid the color of the ribbon, is two or three inches long.

An ordinary book-marker may be properly made from the following directions:

The width of the ribbon is two and a half inches; the length, one yard, after it is finished. To ensure this, a yard and a quarter of ribbon is procured, and a piece of fine linen tightly framed. Upon this, the end of the ribbon, to the depth of ten inches, is to be smoothly tacked at the extreme edges by fine cotton. Along the bottom edge, and across the top of the ten-inch length, the ribbon must also be tacked.

Five inches from the end of the ribbon, the design, traced and cut out in cardboard, is to be fixed with small pins and then sewed down, and embroidered in gold, silver, or purse-silk, according to circumstances. This being done, the work should be covered from dust, and the other end of the ribbon (if the framed linen is large enough to receive both) tacked down and treated precisely similar, only the pattern must be worked on the contrary side of the ribbon, or, as a double marker, it will not hang right when in the book.

When the embroidery is finished, the linen should be cut from the frame, and then from the back of the ribbon close to the work.

To make up the marker, the plain end below the embroidery is to be turned back four and a half inches over the wrong side, leaving half an inch of plain ribbon *below* the design on the right side.

The two edges of the ribbon, to the depth of four and a half inches, are now to be sewn together by the neatest stitches of fine silk the exact shade of the ribbon. The raw edge of the turned up end is to be hemmed across, above the design, by stitches so fine as to be invisible on the right side; and the book-marker, which should now appear as neat on one side as the other, will be ready for the fringe.

A soft-twist silk fringe two inches deep is best, if the embroidery is done in silk. If in gold, a gold fringe is more suitable. Twice the length of the two ends, and three inches over for turnings, is the proper measurement. The fringe should be sewed along one side of the marker singly, and then turned and sewed along the other, so that both sides may be perfectly neat and alike.

Fig. 110.—Design for Alms-Basin Mat.

Figure 110 is a simple and chaste design for a circular mat of velvet to fit the bottom of an alms-dish and deaden the jingling sound of coin upon the bare surface of metal.

The mat should be of velvet, lined with silk, and trimmed with a fringe of gold or silk, as best suits the embroidery, not over an inch deep.

Small articles like these, of suitable materials and careful workmanship, are often most acceptable offerings from those whose limited time or means will not justify their undertaking larger pieces of church work.

A sermon-case is a very useful present for a clergyman, and may be embroidered quite simply, or elaborately, according to the taste and means of the worker. As the same rules and designs will apply to this as to the other articles described, it will be sufficient to give directions for making up the case when worked.

Sermon-cases are made in two ways, either stiff and flat like a book-cover, or firm and soft for rolling.

For the book-cover kind, two sheets of stout cardboard must be cut to the exact size, and joined at the back by a narrow strip of calico pasted along each side. Over this foundation thin lining muslin must be smoothly stitched inside and out; after which the velvet may be tacked evenly on by stitches drawn over the inside edge. A full half inch of velvet should be turned over to make the edges secure.

The silk lining is then to be adjusted and sewed to the velvet with neat stitches, every one of which, if rightly taken, will tend to tighten the material over the mounting-board.

As a finish, a well-made cord of gold or silk, or a mixture of both, is to be sewn all around the case. This cord, which must be about half an inch in circumference, should effectually conceal the stitches uniting the edges of the velvet and silk. A piece of elastic, a quarter of an inch wide, is to be sewed, top and bottom, on the inside of the back, for the sermon to be passed through.

The size of the case must be governed by the size of the sermon-paper used by the clergyman for whom it is intended. Ten inches by eight is a good size for quarto paper.

By using parchment instead of cardboard, and kid or morocco in place of lining muslin, the sermon-case may be made to roll.

DESIGNS ON CARDBOARD.

The use of cardboard designs in church embroidery is a mechanical method of working, but it is also quite an effective one. It is metallic-looking, however, and should not be used in imitations of ancient work. For monograms, letters of texts, and geometrical figures which require clear, sharp outlines, the firm edges of a cardboard foundation will be particularly serviceable.

Embroidery designs to be worked over cardboard must first be traced on thin paper, and then transferred to the cardboard by one of two ways: that of placing the drawing on the cardboard, with black transfer paper between, and tracing it carefully with an ivory stiletto or hard pencil; or by pricking, pouncing, and drawing, as directed for other patterns.

A clear outline of the design having been made on the cardboard, it should be cut out accurately with sharp scissors. In this cutting out, strips of the cardboard, called *stays*, must be left here and there to keep together such parts of the design as would separate or fall away, if the entire outline were cut around; and these stays must not be cut off until the edges of the cardboard pattern are firmly secured on the framed material by close stitches of cotton.

After the stays are removed, if the design is to be raised, one row of even twine should be sewed down along the centre of the figure; it is then to be worked over with the silk. This one row of twine will give to the work the bright sharp effect of gold in relief. *More* than one row would spoil it.

The thickness of the twine must be regulated by the size of the figure to be raised. To raise the embroidery at all is quite a matter of taste, as excellent specimens of work are constantly done over the card alone.

For gold, or gold-color silk embroidery, the upper side of the card foundation should be painted yellow. This can be done by a wash of common gamboge or yellow ochre. The best cardboard for this purpose is that known as thin mounting board.

CHURCH-WORK IN APPLIQUÉ.

This may properly be used for almost any material; and a great deal of church decoration is done entirely by this method.

For letterings, or labels, appliqué is particularly appropriate; and the description of a crimson cloth ground labelled with gold-colored letters will explain the method of doing it.

Stout gray holland a few inches longer than the label is first to be framed and the piece of crimson cloth pasted on it. When this is dry, and while in the frame, the outlines of the label and letters are to be pounced and drawn upon it in Chinese white with a camel's hair brush.

In another frame, a piece of gold-colored cloth is to be prepared on brown holland; and upon this the whole of the letters, or as many as possible, are to be pounced and drawn in India ink. Over the outlines of the letters, a black cord must be closely sewed; and when the frameful is completed in this manner, the holland is to be pasted all over at the back to secure the stitches and make the letters firm.

When quite dry, the holland with the letters may be taken from the frame. They are then to be cut out with sharp nail scissors—leaving the sixteenth of an inch of cloth beyond the black cord everywhere, and laid in their places on the crimson cloth, fixed with pins, and finally sewed down through the black cord by stout *waxed* silk in stitches an eighth of an inch apart. The small edge of gold-colored cloth beyond the cord should not be interfered with; it will rather improve the effect of the letters on the crimson ground.

A black cord must also be closely sewed along the outline of the label, and beyond it a gold silk cord the color of the letters. This done, and the work strengthened at the back by paste, the label may be taken from the frame. It should then be cleanly cut to within an eighth of an inch of its outline all around, when it will present a perfect piece of work of its kind, and will be in a condition to transfer or mount to its final position.

Fig. 111.—PATTERN FOR LINEN ALTAR-CLOTH.

The "fair linen cloth" is laid on the thicker covering at the top, and falls over the table in front to the depth of the worked border, unless there is an embroidered super-frontal beneath, which it would conceal.

It is made of lawn or the finest linen, and bordered with an appropriate design in chain-stitch—which may be worked either with white or colored cotton. This cloth should be long enough either to cover the two sides of the altar; or it may be made only to turn down, as at the front, to the width of the border; which, in every case should be continued along the two ends from the front of the cloth.

The pattern in Figure 111 may be used for white or colored cottons, or for a mixture of both. Crimson and blue are the most suitable colors for embroidering altar-linen. The worked border should rest upon a plain hem an inch deep.

CHAPTER XV.

LINEN LACE-WORK.

MUCH of this is very ancient, and it is often so beautiful that it comes properly under the head of art-needlework.

POINT-CONTÉ,

Best known by its modern name of Guipure d'Art, is almost the only kind of ancient work which, in its modern revival, has retained some degree of beauty.

Ancient guipure was made of thin vellum covered with gold, silver, or silk thread; and the word guipure derives its name from the silk when thus twisted round vellum being called by that name. Cotton afterward replaced the vellum, and several modern laces are known as guipure; but the name is not correct, and is appropriate only to that kind of lace where one thread is twisted round another thread or substance, as in the ancient Guipure d'Art.

This is effected by netting a foundation, and darning a pattern over it with the same linen thread; so that the high-sounding point-conté is simply darned netting. But beautiful effects are produced with it, and it has a look of old church lace.

The groundwork should be netted with linen thread in the shape of a square; and the thread may be coarse or fine according to the purpose for which it is intended. The netting is begun with two stitches, and one is added at the end of every row, until there is one more stitch than is needed for the number of holes. Thus if a square of twenty-six holes is required, increase until there are twenty-seven stitches; then decrease one at the end of every row until only two stitches are left. The last two are knotted together without forming a fresh stitch.

Great care should be taken to have the netting true and even, so that it will stretch properly in the little frame used for the work.

Each corner of the netting should be fastened to the corresponding corner of the frame; and the lacing should be made as tight as possible, as it is much easier to work on than when loose.

The working of the most elaborate patterns in Guipure d'Art

depends entirely upon a mastery of the stitches, of which there is quite a variety. Those in most common use are Point d'Esprit, Point de Toile, Point de Feston, Point de Reprise, Point de Bruxelles, and Wheels and Stars.

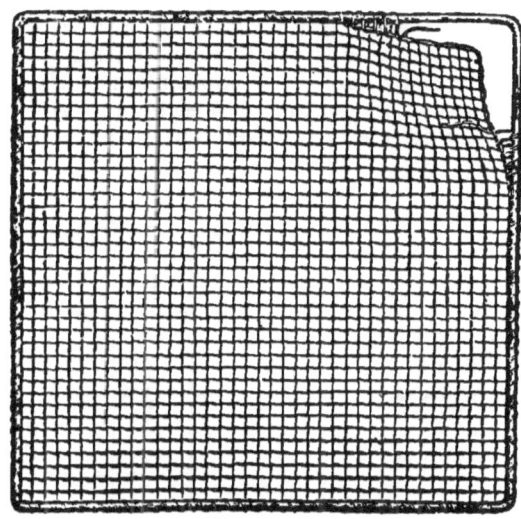

Fig. 112.

Point d'Esprit is a succession of small loops. Beginning in the lower right hand corner of the framed foundation, a row of loops should be worked of the length required; then the frame should be turned, and loops worked on the opposite half of each

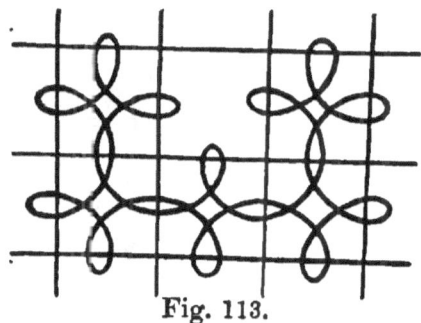

Fig. 113.

square, intersecting the first loops in the centre of each intervening bar of netting. The illustration will make the work quite plain.

This stitch is worked with finer thread than that used in the foundation, No. 10, perhaps, on a netting of No. 6.

POINT DE TOILE, or LINEN STITCH, is merely plain and regular darning over and under each cross thread, making the foundation a closer piece of network. There must be the same number of stitches in each square both ways, to keep the foundation perfectly even; and although the illustration has only four squares within each of the larger ones, it is often made fine enough to contain six or eight.

POINT DE FESTON is done in overcast stitches. At each stitch the frame is turned; the stitches are taken across the square, and increase in length at the top of the square.

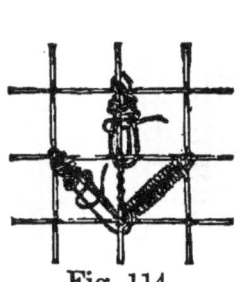

Fig. 114.

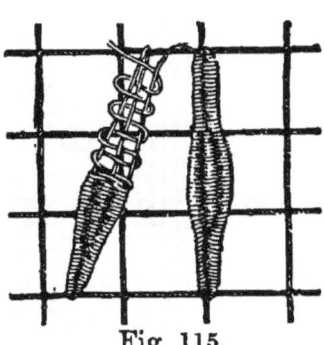

Fig. 115.

POINT DE REPRISE, or DARNING, is begun by stretching two or three threads over one, two, or more squares. The threads are then darned over and under; and the last stitch, while passing through, is

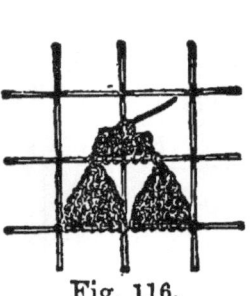

Fig. 116.

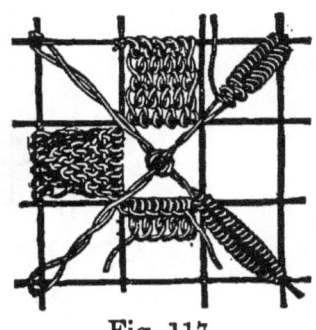

Fig. 117.

arranged with the needle to form the next. This is one of the easiest stitches to learn; and it is always worked with *coarser* thread than the foundation.

POINT DE BRUXELLES is merely a kind of loose button-hole stitch, and is principally used for filling up squares. It will also form leaves when the number of stitches is lessened in each row until they finish off in a point.

WHEELS are begun in the centre. Four threads are taken across, as shown in the first illustration; the thread is twisted in returning to the starting point, and the wheel formed by passing thread under and over the netting and the crossing threads. It is fastened off at the back of the wheel.

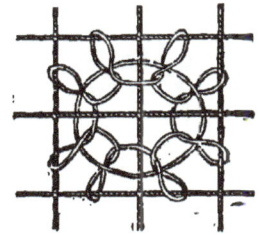   

Fig. 118.—WHEEL BEGUN.   Fig. 119.

The next design is a square wheel. It is worked in the same way as the preceding, with the addition of loops in POINT D'ESPRIT, through which and under and over the cross-twisted threads four or five rows of thread are passed.

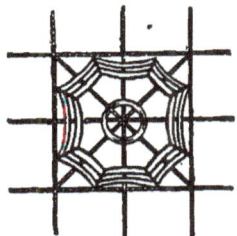

Fig. 120.—SQUARE WHEEL.

STARS are of various forms, as shown in figures.

The first one is worked in POINT DE FESTON around a single square hole, which is filled in by a small wheel, or rosette.

The second is worked alternately in POINT DE FESTON and POINT DE BRUXELLES around a centre crossed by POINT D'ESPRIT threads.

Figure 123 is more elaborate. Begin at the place marked *a* (Figure 124), twist the thread three times round the nearest thread of the netting, draw it on to the knot, *b*; repeat this three times, following the order of the letters; twist the working thread also between the threads, as seen in the illustration, and fasten it underneath the knot, *a*; for the wheel, fasten on the cotton afresh, and work the rest of the pattern in POINT DE REPRISE.

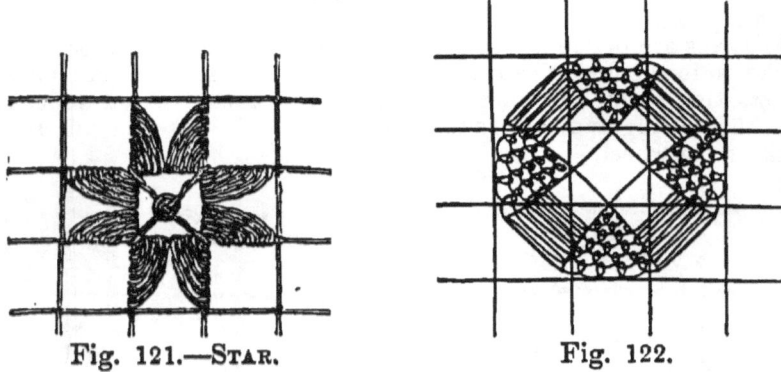

Fig. 121.—STAR.　　　　　　Fig. 122.

The small square is worked on a foundation which is netted over a mesh 2 1-10 inches round; this foundation has seven stitches each way. The embroidery is in DARNING-STITCH, POINT D'ESPRIT, and

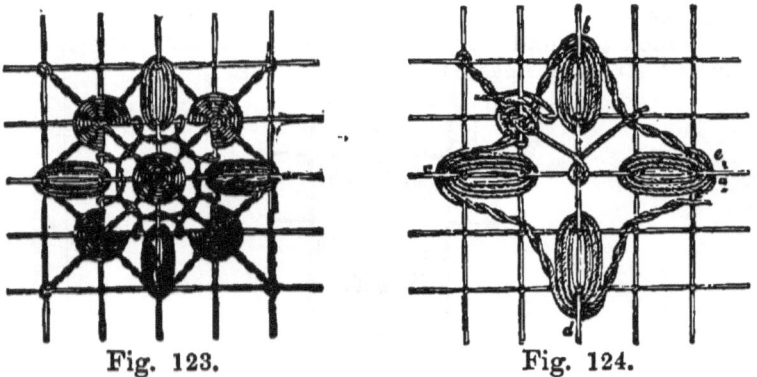

Fig. 123.　　　　　　Fig. 124.

WHEELS. The outer edge is button-holed. Larger squares can be made in the same way, with a few added rows in length and breadth. These pieces are easily joined together with a few stitches.

A quarter of a large square is given on page 121. The outer border is done in POINT D'ESPRIT; next to this there is a border in linen stitch. In each corner there is a large star, which is worked in raised darning-stitch, and fastened to the netting at each point; there is a wheel edged with button-hole stitch in the centre of the star. The pattern for the centre of the square—only a quarter of which is shown in the illustration—consists of four branches forming small

ARTISTIC EMBROIDERY. 121

triangles in Point de Bruxelles, four open-work stars or wheels worked over four holes of the netting, and a four-branched centre of Point de Feston with a wheel in the middle.

Fig. 125.—SMALL SQUARE.

Fig. 127 is a pretty square that has the advantage of being very quickly worked. The border and groundwork are done in Point

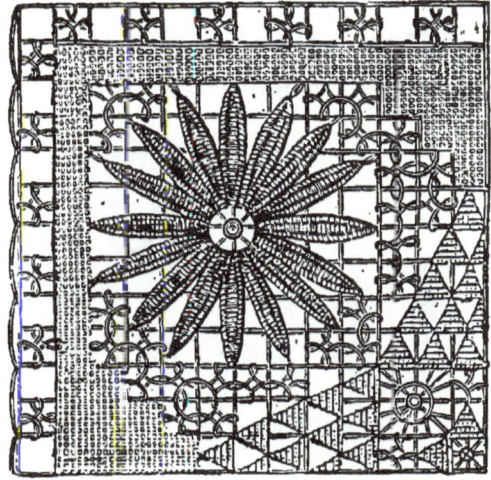

Fig. 126.—QUARTER OF A SQUARE IN GUIPURE D'ART.

d'Esprit, the centre star in Point de Reprise, the pattern in Point de Toile. The four holes in the centres of the darned squares are filled in with wheels.

Small squares are very pretty for cuffs, handkerchiefs, or cravat ends. They are worked with very fine cotton in the same manner as the larger ones, beginning on two stitches in one corner. The different stitches in the two patterns given will be recognized as Point de Feston, Point de Reprise, Point de Toile, and Point d'Esprit.

Fig. 127.—SQUARE FOR ANTIMACASSAR.

The handsome square (Fig. 130), is worked in Point d'Esprit, with an outline edging of Point de Reprise. This part may also be done in close button-hole stitch. The groundwork is in Point de Toile, with

Fig. 128.—SQUARE IN GUIPURE D'ART.

Fig. 129.—SQUARE IN GUIPURE D'ART.

Point de Reprise worked on it. It is very effective, and large and small squares may easily be multiplied by different combinations.

ROSETTES, INSERTIONS, ETC.

The first Rosette is worked in Point de Toile and small wheels. The central wheel is larger, and is ornamented with a round of overcast.

The star-shaped one has a knitted groundwork, which is made by casting on six stitches, joining the stitches in a circle, and knitting in

Fig. 130.—SQUARE IN GUIPURE D'ART.

the first round two stitches in every stitch. For the next eight rounds. two stitches in every increased stitch; in all the other stitches,

Fig. 131.—ROSETTE IN GUIPURE D'ART.

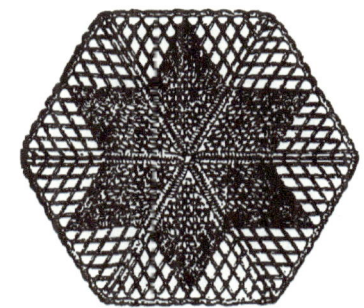

Fig. 132.—ROSETTE IN GUIPURE D'ART.

one stitch. The last, or tenth round, is worked without increasing.

The rosette is then darned in darning-stitch, linen-stitch, and Point d'Esprit. The edge is worked in button-hole stitch, three button-hole stitches to every selvedge stitch.

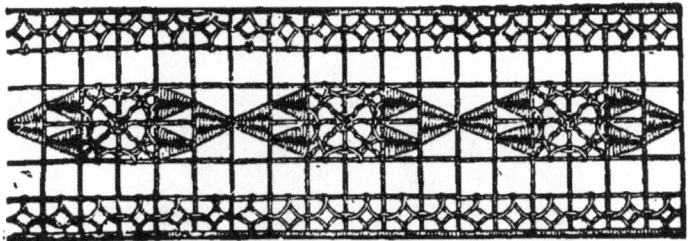

Fig. 133.—INSERTION IN GUIPURE D'ART.

The netted foundation of the inserting pattern is six holes wide. Begin the netting at one corner with two stiches; work five rows, at the end of each of which increase one stitch; continue to work the

Fig. 134.

Fig. 135.

strip with the same number of stitches—alternately decreasing one at the end of one row, and *in*creasing one at the end of the next. To decrease, net two stitches together; to increase, net two in one hole.

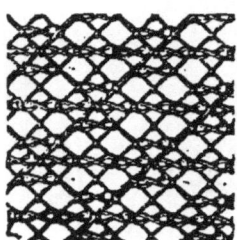

Fig. 136.

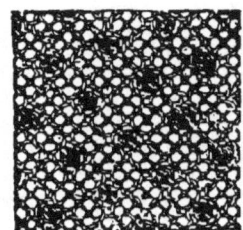

Fig. 137.

When the strip is long enough, finish it by decreasing in the same proportion as the increasing at the beginning.

The pattern is worked in Point de Feston and star-wheel; the border is of Point d'Esprit. The strip is finished on each side with a row of button-hole stitches.

The four patterns given above will be found very useful for filling up small squares, or for varying the groundwork of Point d'Esprit.

Figure 134 is a succession of Point de Feston stitches, which half fill each square of the netting. This pattern, to look well, must be worked very evenly.

Figure 135 is a kind of double Point d'Esprit.

Figure 136 is a twisted thread taken *across* each square, and resembles lace stitches.

Figure 137 is a succession of small, close wheels, mingled with Point d'Esprit. This makes a very effective grounding.

Fig. 138.—FLOWER IN GUIPURE D'ART.

This flower, which can be used for many purposes, is worked in Point de Reprise, and may be done either with linen thread or with purse silk in colors.

The pretty corners for cushions, handkerchiefs, etc., are worked in Point d'Esprit, Linen, and Darning-stitch; and the netted foundation is done by casting on two stitches, and working in rows backwards and forwards—increasing one stitch at the end of every row.

The corner border requires a strip of netting nine squares wide, cut out in vandykes on one side, and worked round in button-hole stitch. The embroidery is done in Darning-stitch, Point d'Esprit, Linen-stitch, bars, and wheels. It is edged with button-hole stitch on the outside, on which is worked a row of crochet-purl.

For this, work one double in every button-hole stitch; after every other stitch draw out the loop on the needle about one-tenth of an inch; take out the needle and leave the loop as a purl; take up one loop in the last double stitch, and cast it off with the next double stitch.

Besides being used for tidies, cushions, etc., this border makes very pretty inserting.

But we must leave the fascinating subject of *Guipure d'Art*, and turn our attention to one or two other kinds of Linen Lace-Work.

POINT COUPÉ,

Or Cut-work, improperly called Greek lace, is made on a foundation of linen, of which some of the threads are cut away and the others worked over, making regular square spaces.

A clearly defined ground plan is thus produced, and the pattern, however rich and varied, is subdued and confined by guiding lines, and may be made to form stars, circles, crosses, or cobwebs, of a geometrical character.

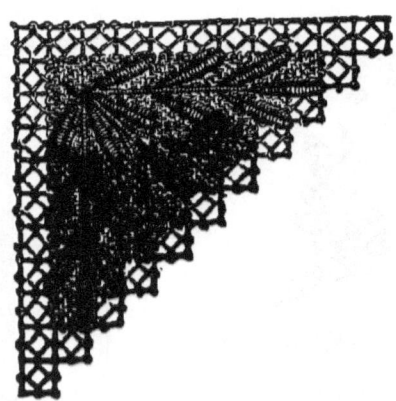 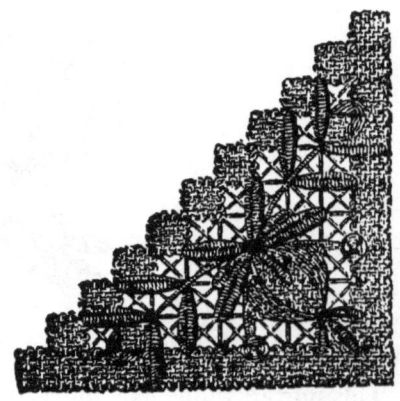

Fig. 139.   Fig. 140.—CORNER BORDERS.

This kind of work is very durable, and has all the respectability of age. Old specimens of it are frequently seen, and the seventeenth century painters were very partial to it, using it for the turned-up cuffs of the vandyke dress, and to edge the falling collars. The finer kinds of it are very laborious, and one beautiful variety wrought on thin linen fabrics is known as Spanish nun-work.

Point Coupé is very effective in furniture decoration, and for this purpose it can scarcely be too coarse. Brown packing-cloth makes a good foundation; worked with brown thread in a suitable pattern, simple enough to be clearly defined by the thick threads, it will make a beautiful border. A Macramé fringe, made of the same thread as that used for the work, will form a pretty finish, if the knotted pattern is simple and unobtrusive, as it should not divide attention with the border, to which it is only an appendage.

ARTISTIC EMBROIDERY.

Cut-work is particularly suitable for the ends of a white linen altar-cloth, worked on stout linen with a thick, soft, white linen thread, and in a very rich pattern. The lace should be firmly finished off with a flat hem of the linen all round, making it complete in itself. A fringe of linen thread is a suitable finish to the Point-Coupé.

After the cover, of finer linen, has been washed and gotten up without starch, the cut-work borders should be sewn on the ends with an open stitch, which may be easily cut when the cloth becomes soiled; which will occur much oftener than with the borders.

Afternoon tea-cloths, cake-covers, etc., may be very prettily ornamented with this linen work. When intended for a border, it should be finished with close button-holing to make it strong.

For a tea-cloth, holland or crash makes a good foundation; and a suitable pattern for this purpose is made by drawing out nine threads each way, and stitching all around the square spaces—taking up three threads with every stitch. In the openings thus made, wheels, stars, or other figures, are worked.

POINT-TIRÉ,

Or drawn-work, is also suited to decorative purposes; it is very simple and easy of execution — being very effective in proportion to the labor spent upon it.

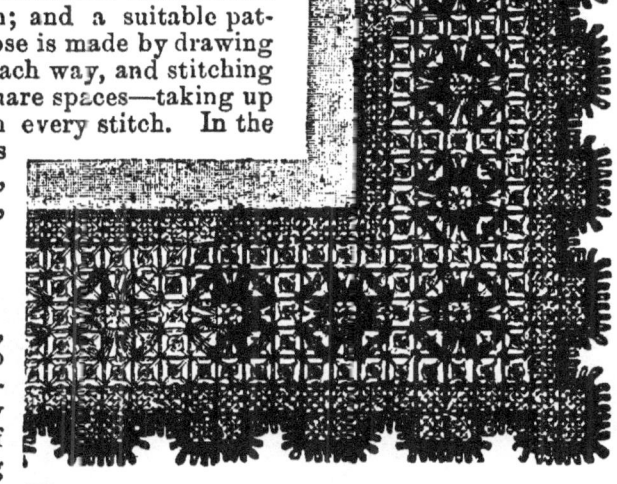

Fig. 141.—Corner Border in Guipure d'Art.

It is an Italian invention, and is very ornamental for the ends of table-cloths, toilet-cloths, tidies, or towels—the last especially being its original use.

Point-tiré is made in the material of the cloth itself; some of the threads being drawn out, and the remainder worked into patterns more or less elaborate. A hem-stitch like that used for pocket-handkerchiefs is useful in this work; it may be done singly along a row of drawn threads, or for a broader line on both sides the row—either taking up the same threads as those taken on the other side, so making little bars, or taking half the threads from each of two of the opposite stitches, and thus forming a zigzag.

Other patterns may be made by passing a thick linen thread along the centre of a row of threads from which the weft has been drawn, and either twisting them over each other or knotting them into groups. It adds to the beauty of an article to embroider the spaces of plain linen between the rows of drawn work, either with silk, or

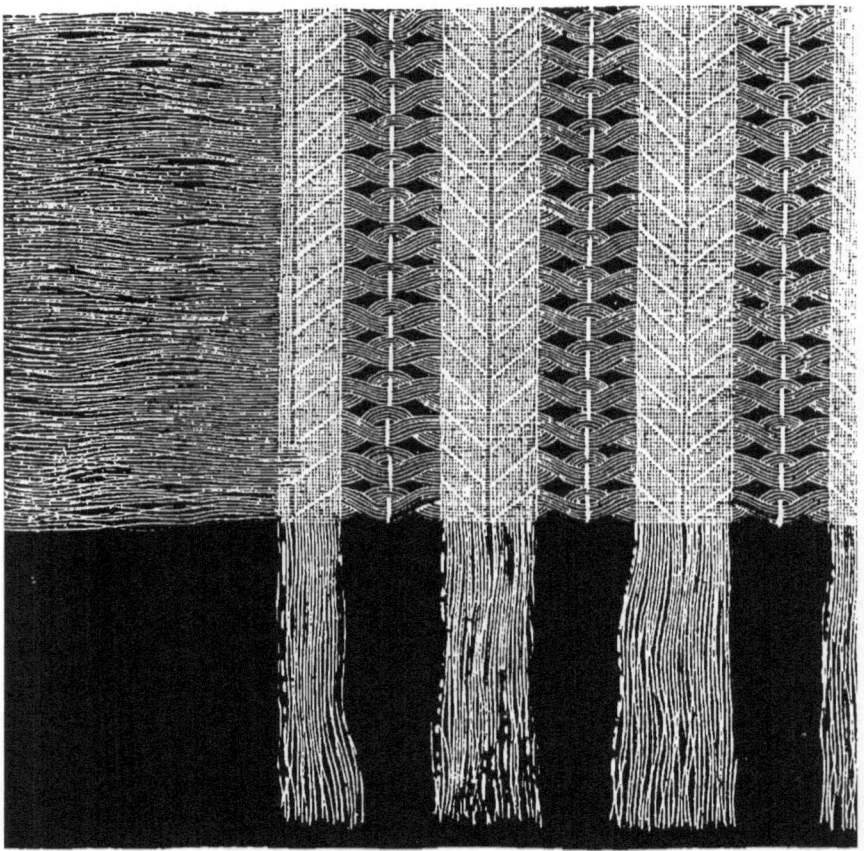

Fig. 142.—COVER FOR A SMALL TRAY.

with red or blue embroidery cotton, mixing a little of whichever is used with the fringe. The patterns should be very simple: line patterns, dots, stars, etc.

Figure 142 is a good specimen of embroidered drawn-work.

The materials used for this cover are white linen and coarse white embroidery cotton. The linen must not be very fine, and it should be of rather loose texture.

When cut to the desired size the first thing to be done is to ravel out the threads for the purpose of forming the fringe, which should be about an inch deep. It should at first be ravelled on only three sides: the selvedge and the two cross sides—the other selvedge side being left until the work is nearly finished.

For the work, draw out twenty-seven threads close together; then leave a space, and draw out twenty-seven more in the same manner. The space from which the threads are drawn is worked in a kind of open-stitch with coarse embroidery cotton. Twelve threads are taken up with the needle, and fixed by a back-stitch. Six threads are dropped; and then again twelve are taken up in the same way as before—thus forming the chain pattern shown in the illustration.

From the middle of the opaque stripe a single thread is drawn, and worked in common hem-stitch; and on each side narrow stripes in satin-stitch form a sort of herring-bone pattern.

The work consists entirely of a series of opaque and open stripes. When the requisite number of stripes is complete, the fringe may be ravelled out on the fourth side, and the cover is finished.

This work washes well; but it should not be starched or ironed. The proper way of doing it up is to pin or baste it flat and tight while wet, upon a board, or the floor, and let it dry.

IMITATION OF ANTIQUE LACE.

A very rich kind of work founded upon old lace is done by drawing patterns on linen and overcasting or button-holing the outlines. The ground between is then cut away, and the patterns enriched with bars, cords, and raised work.

This kind of linen embroidery may be made very beautiful and lace-like; the exquisite patterns of Venetian, rose, raised, or bone point, can easily be reproduced in it, although, while preserving the peculiar beauty of their forms and proportions, they should, to adapt them to this work, be considerably enlarged and their details much simplified. Unless these rules are carefully followed, the linen-work will appear only a coarse and unsuccessful imitation of the original lace.

This work is sometimes outlined with gold thread, which has an exceedingly rich and beautiful effect; and with a lining of amber, or golden-brown satin, a handsome and unique covering may be made for a variety of articles.

www.ingramcontent.com/pod-product-compliance
Lightning Source LLC
Chambersburg PA
CBHW022136160426
43197CB00009B/1304